I FINALLY QUIT
...And So Can You

How To Gain Everything By Quitting

By David "the quitter" Ross

Creative Force Press

I Finally Quit…And So Can You
© 2015 by David Ross
Join David "the quitter" Ross at www.ifinallyquit.com.

This title is also available as an eBook. Visit www.CreativeForcePress.com/titles for more information.

Published by Creative Force Press
4704 Pacific Ave, Suite C, Lacey, WA 98503
www.CreativeForcePress.com

All rights reserved. No part of this publication may be reproduced, stored in a retrieval system, or transmitted in any form or by any means--for example, electronic, photocopy, recording--without the prior written permission of the publisher.

Revised version ISBN: 978-1-939989-24-6
©2015 Original ISBN: 978-1-939989-17-8

Printed in the United States of America

Ready to BREAK FREE from 'bad' habits and pick up 'better' ones?

Then it's time to JOIN the I Finally Quit movement and CONNECT with others doing the same!

www.ifinallyquit.com

This book is for anyone who has ever wanted to break free from making excuses, procrastinating and putting things off, smoking, drinking, being mean, etc…

Anyone who, like me, wants to be…better!

"Dave 'the quitter' Ross is an extraordinary gift to the world. His authentic and transparent journey in *I Finally Quit* of where he's been and what he's learned along the way will inspire millions that they are not alone, and they can move beyond their addictions, too. I am a huge fan of Dave 'the quitter' and his movement."
- Terilee Harrison, International Leadership Coach, Facilitator and Transformational Speaker

"A riveting story, made so much more powerful because it is the true story of a 25-year journey to death's door and the road back."
- K. Holmes, CEO/Founder TEAM Referral Network

"...Once in the trenches, his amazing improvement of lifestyle and health is extraordinary...I believe in *I Finally Quit* and in David."
- Dr. H. K. Tabrizi, MD

"...This is what finally worked for me! Now I'm a quitter too! Thanks IFQ!"
- Stacy F., CPFT, Spencerville Fitness

"Thank you for the inspiration...I finally quit smoking and over-eating."
- Tony, MBA

Table of Contents

Foreword	7
Prologue	9
Introduction	11
Chapter 1: Jump in the Fire	17
Chapter 2: Where Did I Go Wrong?	28
Chapter 3: Somebody to Love	47
Chapter 4: She's Gone	55
Chapter 5: Brother, Can You Spare a Dime?	58
Chapter 6: Sweet Sister Mercy	62
Chapter 7: That's It, I Quit. I'm Movin' On	71
Chapter 8: Sanitarium	83
Chapter 9: Oops!...I Did it Again	86
Chapter 10: Way Down in Old Indiana	93
Chapter 11: Running Scared	99
Chapter 12: Travelin' Man	103
Chapter 13: Must Have Gotten Lost	110
Chapter 14: All I Ever Wanted Was a Place to Call My Own	117
Chapter 15: Ain't it the Truth	120
Chapter 16: Recovery	136
Chapter 17: What a Long, Strange Trip It's Been	144
Chapter 18: On the Road Again	149
Chapter 19: Home Sweet Home	153
Chapter 20: Where Do We Go from Here?	155
Epilogue: Thanks	158
What is the I Finally Quit Movement?	161
About the Author	163
Supporters	164

Foreword

From the personal physician of David "the quitter" Ross:

No doctor can claim that he or she remembers all of their patients equally. No matter what, some patients have stories and histories that stand out. Unique patients make a deep impact in a doctor's memory and soul. David has been one of those great stories that I tell other patients about, without mentioning his identity, of course.

I first saw David in my office in April of 2010. He was not feeling great during this visit. He was shaky, had shooting pain in his legs, and his face would go partially numb every now and then. Exams and lab results revealed his liver enzymes were elevated. But it would still be more than a year before I would see him again...fighting for his life.

He seemed to have "curtains" over his eyes, almost like a block to the truth. He was not "there" yet, meaning David was not seeing the problem yet. He was not aware that the booze he was consuming was slowly taking away his life. We touched upon the subject, and I recommended to him that he quit drinking and offered help, but again he was not "there" yet. He came in one other time for a minor skin problem before his life-threatening experience in 2011.

In September that same year, after his admittance and eight days in the Intensive Care Unit, I saw a new person in front of me. He was still very weak from a rapid weight loss, but he had a big smile and determination in his eyes. This past three years since, I have watched an evolution from a shaken and broken man to a healthy, sober, and productive person.

I remember the day David came to see me to talk about his new goals, especially his goal to help other people quit things that were causing them harm in *their* lives. He was determined to share his journey with others. Stories with happy endings like his are not common, unfortunately.

Drugs, alcohol, and other unhealthy habits consume the lives of millions of people all over the world. But, I believe the *I Finally Quit* website and David's book will be practical tools to help people like him to connect and get support.

David has been in the trenches, and his amazing improvement of lifestyle and health are extraordinary. It has been my pleasure to be his physician, and I hope his awesome transformation is contagious.

Dr. H. K. Tabrizi
San Diego, California

Prologue

Before I get too far with my story, let me tell you that you shouldn't be reading this book. Seriously, this book was never supposed to be written. I wasn't *supposed* to be here. I should have been dead long ago, or in jail. The fact that I am able to share my story with you is not only gratifying, but extremely humbling. I am honored to tell it.

I mentioned I wasn't supposed to be here...well, I most definitely should not have rebounded from an EIGHT day stay in an Intensive Care Unit back in 2011, caused by acute, necrotizing pancreatitis, liver and kidney failure followed by a system-wide infection of *C. difficile*. Three of those eight days, I was kept in a medically induced coma! Yeah...those are a few difficult terms to say...even more difficult to experience. If you are not a doctor or nurse and you didn't follow all of that, it's okay...at the time, I didn't understand it either. What all that means is my pancreas (the gland that assists in digestion and makes insulin to control the body's sugar level) was dying and my liver and kidneys were shutting down. The doctors kept me heavily sedated to numb me from the pain and give my body a chance to heal. I also had a disgusting infection from a bacteria (*C. difficile*), that kills approximately 30,000 inpatients of hospitals every year. Here I was completely septic (massive infection), walking around with that infection and damaged organs for who knows how long.

I shouldn't have lived after taking the worst hit in a four car pile-up in 1994. I should have been a casualty of drinking and driving or wound up in jail for vehicular manslaughter, with as many times as I drove drunk and made poor decisions. I shouldn't have the story I'm about to tell you, but God had other plans. You will see His hand and protection in the stories I'm about to reveal. My strongest desire is that you will be inspired throughout the telling and recounting of these actual, unembellished series of events. Through that inspiration, I hope you can QUIT whatever is holding you back – *whatever* it is.

It doesn't matter if it's something you struggle with out in the open (like drinking or drugs) that everyone knows you struggle with (and believe me…they know, even if you don't think they do). It also doesn't matter if it's something you have been able to conceal, like shame or guilt. If my story doesn't give you what you are looking for, I hope someone else on the IFQ (I Finally Quit) website has a story that will.

I'm thankful and honored to be able to share my story with you. Without exaggeration, I can honestly tell you I've cheated death nearly as many times as a cat. Before I use up that proverbial *ninth life*, let me tell you a little bit of how I got *here*, how you came to pick up this book, and what I've spent numerous days and nights to build in order to give everyone a place to go when they need inspiration.

Introduction

August 8, 2011...

Two nurses quickly attach leads to my chest, the monitor is beeping and I know I will be taken care of. I give the quick recap of the meal that led to all of this, still hoping for a food poisoning diagnosis, but knowing better. One nurse asks me if I have been drinking today. "Of course not," I reply. *It is only the early afternoon*, I remember thinking. I have completely forgotten about the copious amounts of bourbon at 8am and the rum at 9am. Besides, as much as I drink and with my tolerance for alcohol, that is clearly not the problem here.

After 15-20 minutes of extremely close monitoring, it is determined that I do have an irregular heartbeat, but I am not having a heart attack. I am moved to another examination area. Another nurse is getting me situated and hooked up to the monitors in this area. Blood is being drawn, oxygen tubing is placed in my nose and the question is asked again, "How much have you had to drink today?" "Nothing today," I let her know. Again, I am not intentionally lying, I am unaware of just how bad things have gotten and not really grasping the severity of what has happened over the last few hours.

My mind is struggling to keep up with how I got "here" – not just the emergency room in San Francisco 750 miles away from where my day started, but "here" as in…life. As my body and internal organs are shutting down, the details may not be all that important. I'm trying to keep calm as the next 25 minutes are filled with nurses and technicians coming in and out of the trauma unit. I know I'm dying.

Deep down, I've actually known it for quite some time. It's not even the first time in my life I've known Death has come for me. *"I'm still not ready to go,"* I think to myself, but the thought of the pain leaving me if I just accept this fate is pretty tempting. I wonder to myself if anyone would really miss me if I die right here, right now. These dark thoughts and almost accepting this fate were put on hold, as some of the test results began coming in. The results would inform the emergency room doctor and nurses who were working to keep me *here* that my internal organs were shutting down.

They were stunned to see this much damage done to someone not even 40 years old. The doctor says he believes I am in this position due to severely abusing alcohol. Again, I let them know I haven't been drinking, but just then, in that moment, I realize it wasn't just today's damage. I've been drinking non-stop for nearly 25 years…and for the first time in more than a decade, I have an honest conversation about my drinking.

In this book, I am going to reveal to you how I was able to walk away from my cigarette smoking addiction of 20 years, my alcohol drinking addiction of 25 years, and other vices that held me back. At my most addicted, I was smoking nearly two packs and drinking a fifth of bourbon nearly every day for five years. I am going to reveal how I arose from a sedentary, couch-potato lifestyle to take control of my life, fitness, and health, and then to triumphantly declare, "I *Finally* Quit!"

You will get a front row seat to witness how an addict with a compulsive personality rechanneled his focus to build an online army of quitters. I will be candid and reveal how nearly every experience I had, decision I made, and situation I was in prior to August 2011 was influenced or dominated by my commitment to alcohol. I didn't know it while I was "in it," but my commitment level to booze surpassed everything – friends, family, work, fiancé, residence, and more. Nothing in my life was as important as my next drink or my next cigarette. Booze and cigarettes were front and center in my life.

I'm here to tell you, it wasn't easy and there were several times I sat with my face in my hands wondering how I had let myself reach such horrible lows, and I wanted to just give up and take my own life. Ultimately, I said to myself, *"Enough is enough, and I've reached the point I will not tolerate this anymore,"* and I quit…I quit the detrimental actions and behaviors that repeatedly led to negative circumstances. I am here to tell you quitting is far more difficult than giving up.

It would take me another three years before I realized my sleepless nights — to "get just one more thing right" — were fueling a desire to have others share in the feeling of quitting. Even sober, addicts sometimes make questionable decisions. At my core, that's who I am – a compulsive addict. The word *addict* is easy for some to understand or even associate with. As people, we can be addicted to just about anything – some good and some bad. The compulsive aspect seems a little more difficult for most people to understand. To this day, although I no longer drink or smoke, I still feel "irresistible urges" that go against what I know I should or shouldn't be doing.

This book and the creation of the IFQ membership website are two perfect examples of my compulsive and addictive personality or traits. I spent countless hours and more money than I'd care to admit in bringing them from my mind into the real world.

In building and creating ifinalllyquit.com and I Finally Quit, Inc., I discovered that I would make some things easy and some things difficult for myself. All the while, I was compelled to keep going. What compelled me? My need for perfection? My desire to matter? My want to see the world a better place? My goal to see others feel what I felt the moment, the week after, the months and years after saying, "I Finally Quit"? Yes, all of those, but most of all, my addiction to wanting everyone's short period of time on this planet to be the best for them *and* those around them.

I sincerely hope you'll see my story for what it is – a cautionary tale. I hope you will quit any bad behaviors you may have BEFORE you allow them to cause you to lose important people, that job or income, or even the roof over your head. I was so addicted to finding my next drink with what seemed like an endless budget – until it wasn't endless. I lost (and more accurately chased away) people around me, a great job and income, and yes…even the roof over my head. It has been said that hindsight is 20/20, and to most of us…it is. So please, take this book for what it is – it's your glasses, or better yet, it's your LASIK surgery for a glimpse into the future. What will you do with it? I know what I'd like to see for you.

I encourage you to quit smoking, BEFORE the inevitable heart attack, cancer, or disease comes. I encourage you to quit drinking, BEFORE the organ failure, jail time, or homicide. I encourage you to quit overeating, BEFORE obesity leads to illness or death. I encourage you to QUIT!

The great news is I Finally Quit…and so can you! The even better news is I went on to build a social network for quitters. Through the interactive website, it's simple to become part of the *I Finally Quit* community. Once registered, there are groups created for people to join, whether they want to quit procrastinating, quit bad attitudes, quit smoking, or end bad relationships. Through the IFQ website, I'm happy to say, "There's a group for that."

Please take a moment right now and visit www.ifinallyquit.com, and join this army of determined quitters.

1

Jump in the Fire

It's a miracle you're even reading this. I mentioned taking the worst of a four car pile-up – check this out. For real…I was hit by a semi-truck, then a Monte Carlo, both of which were travelling over 50 miles an hour when they struck my stationary vehicle, as I sat inside. Like I said…I wasn't *supposed* to be here and you weren't *supposed* to have this book in your hand. Or, are you? By the time you are done reading this intro, you are going to be saying, "No way," out loud…I promise.

October 1994 set off a series of events that still makes me shake my head to this day. I was privileged and honored to be the best man in a wedding that day, all those years ago. Later in this true story, you'll come to see that the real "best man" turns out to be my friend, the groom, not me. I can call this man a true friend, and I am incredibly honored to know him. But for now, here's what happened back then, when the first real domino was tipped over, leading to the next, and the next, and the next…

During the wedding reception, I was a *hot mess*. That phrase hadn't even come into existence yet, but in retrospect, it truly defined me at the time. I'd had way too much beer and bourbon to drink, especially to be around all of the emotions taking place at this wedding and party. You see...love WAS in the air. It was palpable. The love that these two had was so obvious. What was also obvious to me at the time was how much I missed my ex-girlfriend. Oh...did I mention she was *in* the wedding party, too? Being around her, seeing her, and knowing that I missed her tremendously was just too much for me to deal with, so I drank even more.

You see, that is what I and many other drinkers do: we consume alcohol to "numb ourselves" from the feelings and emotions that actually make up the human experience. But, there I was...consuming away, but I needed some air. I just had to get away for a few minutes, so I jumped in my car and went for a drive...while intoxicated.

As I drove more than 15 miles from New Haven, Indiana, to Fort Wayne, Indiana, to see my sister at the restaurant where she was working at the time, I felt relieved to be out of the wedding scene for a bit. However, I definitely should *not* have been behind the wheel of a car at the time. I'd driven to this particular restaurant many times and knew the route like the back of my hand, but that evening I was distracted.

I kept thinking of my ex-girlfriend at the reception and how I should have and could have been a better man and boyfriend for her. My left turn was coming up, so I put my turn signal on and started to veer left ever so slightly to enter the left turn lane. The problem was the signal up ahead was still that...up ahead. I had to jerk the wheel to the right to avoid entering the center median and wrecking my car. And, I can tell you at 6'-6" tall driving a 1994 Ford Festiva (yeah...that's a little car), the last thing I wanted was to be involved in an accident while behind the wheel of that tiny vehicle.

When I swerved to get back into the driving lane, I didn't quite get over far enough and ended up hitting the cement curb or protector of the center median, instantly causing two flat tires on the left side of the vehicle. Not only was I putting lives at risk by driving while intoxicated, but now I was losing control of the vehicle due to the flat tires on the driver's side. I was able to keep the car on the road long enough to get into the real turn lane and make the left turn I thought I was making a few seconds earlier. With the restaurant in sight, I realized the car wasn't going to make it, so I pulled into a different parking lot just prior to the restaurant. I abandoned the car and walked the rest of the way. I still think back to what a sight that must have been, had anyone been around to see it. A tall man in a fancy tux getting out of a tiny car with two flat tires, and just walking away, as if I had arrived at my true destination.

Entering the restaurant, my sister was surprised to see me, as she knew I should still be at the reception of my best friend's wedding. After guzzling down some top-shelf bourbon AND telling her about my faux paus on the way over, somehow I convinced her to give me the keys to her car so I could return to the party I'd left an hour before. When I returned to the reception, my emotional state had not improved.

> **Somehow I convinced my sister to give me her car keys, and my ex to talk with me.**

Somehow I was able to convince my ex that we should have a conversation the following week about getting back together. I wish I could tell you that everything worked out for everyone involved and the story book, fairy tale ending happened right then and there, but it didn't.

As I mentioned, this was just the first domino to fall. The next morning I'd be 20+ miles away, back at home and have to get right back up to Fort Wayne to address my car situation. Like the slow "tick, tick, tick, tick" of a rollercoaster car climbing to the top of the ride, it would be a while before I made the turn; before finding myself in a freefall.

Remember my ex-girlfriend I mentioned from the wedding the night before? She drove me back up to Fort Wayne on what would turn out to be a fateful Monday morning. Before picking up my car, we stopped for lunch to have a conversation about how I was out of control and how my commitment to drinking had driven a wedge between us. Later in the book, I'll reveal just how much I was drinking at this relatively early age and over the next 20 years, it would increase to staggering—no pun intended—levels. She was right, I had to do better, especially since I was no longer going to go to medical school. During my senior year of college, I had decided medicine wasn't the right career path for me. In reality, God had a different plan for me that would take more than two decades for me to see.

During our lunch, I let her know I had to figure out what to do with my life, and I had to find a better way to do it. Feeling pretty good about the progress I seemed to be making, we both left lunch feeling hopeful we could reconcile. I could refocus on my future now that college was behind me. Ready for a week on the road with my travelling sales position, I got in the car—new tires and all—and set off on US 30 from Fort Wayne, Indiana, to Toledo, Ohio.

It was a beautiful mid-October day on the eastern side of Northeast Indiana, and not a cloud in the sky. It must have been about 70 degrees and absolutely perfect for a drive. My windows were down just a smidge to get fresh air into the car and push out the cigarette smoke that billowed from me like a factory's chimney. Back then, at age 22, I was smoking about a pack to a pack and a half a day. I just remember thinking how beautiful the sky was that day.

You know the days where the sky seems to have just the slightest bit of white at the horizon mixing in with the blue sky, then having the blue get just a bit darker all the way across the sky? And, the temperature…it was just perfect. I don't recall what was playing on my CD player, but I can tell you I was probably loving it. I loved having music playing as I drove. My love of thumping bass and driving guitar riffs were a couple of the reasons I was driving such a small car back then.

A few months prior, I had received a check worth several thousands of dollars from my auto insurance company. They sent the check to replace my previous car, which I had driven off the road and into flood waters. Yes, I was drunk at the time and had somehow gotten away with it. As the car literally sank, my best friend and I had to escape from the car and swim to safety. Yet another time of cheating death. I took that insurance check and bought the biggest, loudest stereo available on the market at the time and put it into the smallest car I could fit in. Rock music never sounded so good!

Back to the perfect weather and the perfect driving music on that day in October of 1994. I was driving on a beautiful, wide-open stretch of US 30. This particular section is a four-lane highway: two eastbound and two westbound lanes separated by 15-20 feet of perfectly green grass. It's an area where you can get some real thinking done, as there is very little traffic to distract a person.

Up ahead, maybe about a mile or so, I noticed the horizon had a slightly different look, unlike anything I'd ever seen before. As I got just a little closer, I realized it was smoke...yep...smoke rising into that perfect blue sky. The closer I got to it, the more I could tell what was going on. As it all began to really come into focus, I could see there was a field up ahead on my right that was on fire, and the breeze was causing the smoke to blow across the highway. A soybean field was ablaze. Northeast Indiana and Northwest Ohio at the time grew tons of soybeans not meant for human consumption, which means the farmers allowed them to dry out completely before harvesting. I would find out weeks later that the farmer also harvested natural honey. Smoke is used to get the bees away from the honey, and the farmhands had lost control of their fire, which quickly swept across the dry bean field. More dominos had fallen, and more were coming...

Back to my drive, I could see cars coming out of the smoke on the westbound lanes and cars travelling the same direction as me were heading into the smoke. It looked danger-free, as cars drove into and then out of the smoke. As I approached the smoke, I slowed from about 65 miles an hour down to about 50 by the time I entered the smoke. It quickly became apparent that I would not just whip right through like I thought, as the smoke was much thicker and denser than it had first appeared. Within a couple of quick seconds, I could no longer see the hood of my little car. Visibility was so bad, I literally could not see just a couple of feet in front of me. Panic set in just a bit, but there wasn't anything I could do except keep driving and hope I would exit the thick smoke in just another second or two. It turned out not another full second would pass and I would be trapped in that smoke for the next couple of hours.

In that instant, the only thing that pierced through the smoke were two red lights elevated just above my line of sight. They were the brake lights of a Pontiac minivan, whose driver had come to a full stop in the middle of the highway, and as soon as my mind figured out what my eyes were seeing, it sent a message to my right leg to "stand" on the brakes of my car. I stomped so hard on the brake pad that I was surprised my foot didn't smash through the floor board. The sound of the impact my car made with the stopped minivan in front of me was drowned out instantly by the pain radiating from my right leg.

Instantly, I knew my femur was broken. With my medical background of working at a hospital and my pre-med studies over the past four years, one thing was sure...a broken femur — the longest bone in the body — is no good. The damage done to the surrounding tissues and muscles from this type of fracture can kill a person due to loss of blood and internal bleeding. My eyes followed the pain coming from my right side, and as they saw the two right turns in my upper leg, I confirmed what I already knew…my leg was broken. By the time I would make it to the hospital, my right leg was five inches shorter than my left, as the bone tore through my muscles.

Before I really had time to fully process my situation, reality set in. I knew whoever was coming behind me was going to make impact, as I had with the minivan just a few short seconds ago. It was inevitable. Just as I never really saw the minivan I'd just collided with, whoever was coming behind me was not going to see me either. My instinct was to get out of the car as quick as possible.

> Whatever was coming behind me was going to make impact. It was inevitable.

I pulled at the handle repeatedly, trying to open the door so I could escape the impending impact. However, my driver side door was jammed from the impact of hitting the minivan in front of me. The door just would *not* open. I kept trying, but it wouldn't budge. It was for the best I suppose, as there was no way I was going to be able to run or walk with a broken femur.

This was it, I thought, *I am going to die*. The only thing that made sense in that exact moment was I needed to have my last cigarette, before I died. As if I were about to face a firing squad, I wanted my "last" cigarette. *Yep, I was truly addicted*. My pack was out of reach though. The impact had caused my pack of cigarettes to settle on the passenger side floor and with my right leg broken, I couldn't adjust my weight or reach to get them. As if facing a firing squad albeit without my last cigarette, I refused a blindfold and stared at the rearview mirror. Whatever was coming, I was going to face it head on. I sat staring at the rearview mirror, and nothing could have prepared me for what I saw next.

As I saw the front of the semi-truck that was about to make contact with the rear of my car, a greyscale rainbow of Polaroid-type snapshots of my life passed before my eyes. In what must have been milliseconds, every highlight and milestone of my life whipped right past me as the truck hit the right rear side of the back of my car. I had heard of people saying they "saw their life pass before their eyes," and I had truly just witnessed that phenomenon. Thankfully, the driver of the semi-truck had the foresight to realize he couldn't see anything and had to get off of the highway. He had already begun braking and veering toward the right side of the road, but it was estimated he was still travelling more than 50 miles an hour at the time of impact.

As he made contact with the back of my vehicle, I was forced into the minivan ahead of me, again. Although not a direct, flush collision with the rear of the car, more damage was done to me, my car, and the minivan at that time. I saw the semi go by the right side of my car and the minivan pull away. The truck had nowhere to go but by me, and the lady driving the minivan with four (yes, four) children in front of me decided she couldn't jeopardize them any further. So there I sat…alone with my thoughts, feeling incredibly vulnerable. There was time for prayer, but I'm not even sure to this day if I utilized it. I like to think I did, but reality is, I might not have.

Even though I'd impacted the minivan twice and been hit by a semi, I was very aware of the situation, a little bloodied and thankful to be alive. It's amazing how much one can think and *see* in mere seconds. My analytic mind was in overdrive. It was kind of like putting together an equation and trying to solve it, like A+B=C. On one side of the equation I knew I had struck a minivan, broken my leg, been trapped in my vehicle and hit by a semi-truck, all while being denied my *last* cigarette (we'll call that "A" of that equation) and before I could continue building this equation so I could try to solve it, I was caught completely off guard.

The Monte Carlo's impact with the rear of my car was so forceful that a couple of my ribs broke and the backseat came completely flush with the back of my driver's seat. I never even saw her nor did that driver see me. She would later tell investigators she never even touched the brakes. It was a direct hit at approximately 70 miles an hour. The collision was so forceful that the rear bumper of my car was pushed beyond my rear axle, driving the back seat completely flush with the front seats. Had anyone been in the back seat, there would have been no saving them.

My car spun a couple of times across the two lanes of the highway, before dropping down the 3 or 4 foot embankment of the field on fire. I was now directly *on* the field that was already in flames. These desiccated soy beans I mentioned earlier grow 2-3 feet tall, so the tops of the flames were at eye level for me, just outside of my window. I quickly got back to that "equation" I had been working on and updated it accordingly. So, it was *A* plus *B*; *B* now being I've been rear ended twice and was staring at flames completely surrounding my car. Because of the two impacts to the back of my car where the gas tank is, AND these flames completely surrounding me, the only logical solution to my equation was *C* equaled my car was going to explode. *What a way to go*, I thought. *Would I feel it? Would it be quick?* And then I saw...him.

A man was walking through the flames near the front of my (now even smaller) car. The technology and design that went into this vehicle amazed me, as it folded up like an accordion, protecting me. I raised my voice, not quite yelling, "I'm alive in here. I need some help." He approached my window and said, "Be still. Help is on the way." "On the way? *You* are here now,"

I said. He had one more response for me before he walked away, leaving me all alone…this time he said, "Don't be afraid. Help is on the way." That was it. Just like that, he walked away.

> "Don't be afraid. Help is on the way."

Within seconds, three more men showed up wielding fire extinguishers and blowing fire-killing gas all around my car. As they worked tirelessly to keep the flames away from my car, I *relaxed* the best I could, feeling my life had somehow been spared. I would stay in the car for more than an hour as first-responders tried to figure out how to get me out of the car and to the hospital, where I desperately needed surgical attention.

The helicopter that had been summoned to my location couldn't land close enough to be of value due to the smoke, so I waited for an ambulance to drive me away from the Indiana-Ohio border. By the time I was cut out of the car with the "jaws of life" and driven back to the nearest hospital, like I mentioned, my right leg was five inches shorter than my left. It was a *serious* injury. I was taken to surgery after CAT scans of my abdomen; scans to make sure my vital organs had not suffered major trauma as well. I am thankful to say, the surgery was a success. I still have the metal rod inside my femur.

The recovery time for that surgery required a seven-day stay in the hospital. On day four, the volunteer firemen that had kept the fire away from my car and prevented it from exploding with me still in it, came to visit. I remember being so thankful and grateful to these brave men who went running into a fire to save a complete stranger.

As we quickly bonded and recounted the events of that afternoon, I thought for sure they were putting me on when they kept telling me it was just the three of them in the field that day. I kept asking who the fourth man was…you know, the first one who came up to me and told me to *be still*. They blankly kept looking at each other and started to think I was the one joking and kidding with them. We agreed to disagree, but I *knew* (and still know to this day) there was a fourth. It would take nearly two years for me to really grasp what had happened when the man in the field approached me. Have you said "No way!" yet? If not, it may be coming shortly.

Although already "saved" by asking Jesus into my heart during my teenage years, I'd never read the Bible front to back, just a verse here and there. About a year after this auto accident, I would team up with a sales partner who, 20 years earlier, was a "tent" preacher (an evangelist who would preach an "end times" message from city to city). He was convinced God had spared me for a reason, and strongly encouraged me to get a better understanding of God's Word.

When I read in the book of Daniel about king Nebuchadnezzar commanding Shadrach, Meshach, and Abednego to be put to death in a burning fiery furnace, the story had my attention. Especially when the king wondered why there were four men (not three) loose and not bound in the fiery furnace and the "form of the fourth was like the Son of God." I was filled with tears and thankfulness to God for sparing me. People who I told that story to on a nearly daily basis for years (before and after my reading of the third chapter of Daniel), would tell me God had sent a Protector for me that day. I was destined to do something big someday, they would say.

As you will find out, as my story continues, God's plan would take nearly two decades to unfold and for me to become "the quitter." You will see Him protecting me, even during my homeless stint, making sure I got to tell His story of protection and deliverance. So, strap in and hold on. We've got a lot to cover in a short period of time!

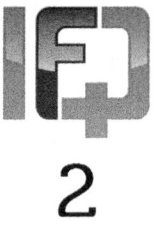

2

Where Did I Go Wrong?

August 8, 2011 (Phoenix)
8:00 AM

I'm waiting for my car service to come pick me up at my friend's apartment, where I've been staying for just a couple of months. But, even during those months, I have really only "been there" a few days, physically and coherently. I travel so much...I'm in a different city across the U.S. nearly every day. I'm really just using her apartment as a place to keep my last few belongings. *I am so happy to have signed a new lease this past weekend to get my own apartment*, I think to myself. It's hard to believe it has been over five years since I had a place to call my own.

I have been extremely irresponsible over that time period, and I alone am to blame. However, some of my friends and family enabled me along the way. Five years earlier, I went broke. With no money, big debt, no apartment or car, I'd been "couch surfing" across the country until recently. Although different friends and family members were able to open their homes to me for most of that time, the fact was...*I had been homeless*, I think to myself. Now, with a successful career again, although not necessarily *needed*, I had the opportunity to get my own place.

My own apartment again...wow, I think...but for now, I need to get back to the airport. It seems as if I'm in airports all the time. Actually, I'm in them several times a week. My driver should be here in just a few minutes. It doesn't leave me too much time to suck down a couple of 50mL bottles of bourbon. You know the ones...the little bottles served on airplanes. I have already gotten two down without my friend even knowing. She knows I drink, heck, *everyone knows* I drink...few know just how much though. I feel as if me drinking to excess is expected at this point. Even so, I don't necessarily want her to know I will have had four of these bottles before 8:30 am, especially considering I didn't go to bed until 1am, due to trying to finish off yesterday's fifth of bourbon! Four...before 8:30 am! That's more than social drinkers would have in one night...and I'm about to have that down before breakfast. I hear the Town Car's horn honk downstairs, and I have got to go!

As I sit in the back seat, I feel great. Actually, the truth is, I'm a little buzzed already, *or is it still,* I wonder to myself. After all, it's only 8:15 am or so. Work has been very profitable as of late. I am a seminar leader, teaching business concepts to doctors and their staff. I am in a different city every day. I'm making enough money that I have hired an assistant to travel with me. He's actually on the way to the airport in his home city of Los Angeles at the same time I'm on my way to Phoenix International.

> I'm a little buzzed already...or is it *still?*

This is my third attempt in the last year to have a traveling assistant. It's a grueling schedule leading seminars everyday across the country and not everyone can keep up with the demands of the road. Now that I am drinking at least a fifth of bourbon every day, the demands of this type of travel is nearly impossible for me to do alone. This current assistant has been great, so far. One of the biggest advantages for me is no longer having to drive, at all. Nowadays, I pretty much take taxis and car services everywhere I go, and now even for work. *Life is good...finally!*

It's been a crazy struggle with tons of self-imposed setbacks over the last five or six years, from losing everything and having a food budget of $10.00 per week to live on, all the way to having unlimited food and drink at my disposal. With the last six years behind me, it's time to focus on the here and now. Speaking of the here and now, with the insane and disgusting events of this last weekend now behind me (more on that in a minute), I take comfort knowing I'll soon be getting my own apartment after more than five years of being homeless...I rest a little easier in the back seat.

As I drink bourbon on the rocks from a disposable coffee cup in the back of the Town Car at 8:15 am, I am thankful and grateful I no longer have to drive. Not driving allows me to do what's become increasingly more and more important to me over the years, and that is consume copious amounts of bourbon. I drink...a lot. Driving for me has become cumbersome. Cumbersome? No, downright scary. As a matter of fact, I am afraid of a lot of different things. I am afraid of bridges, sudden sounds, my thoughts...*everything*. I'm so afraid, I actually shake almost all the time. People can see it. Some have asked about it and want to know if I have a medical condition, but the truth is...I am afraid. I didn't used to be this way, so having drivers and an assistant helps have fewer things to worry about. Worry...that is a better word. I worry about everything.

I make a quick call to my assistant, already boarding his flight at LAX en route to San Francisco. He'll arrive before me, but shouldn't have to wait too long. As we compare itineraries, it appears he'll arrive just about an hour before me. This will be his first trip with me to the Bay Area. I let him know that we stand to make a lot of money this week, which we both really need. The excitement is building for both of us. At the time, had you asked either of us what the worst possible outcome of this day could be...neither could have come up with what awaited: one of us being stranded hundreds of miles from home and the other fighting for his life.

8:30 AM

I have arrived at the airport and am making my way through security. As I put my shoes, belt, laptop, etc., in all the proper bins, I get to my one quart bag. It has been months since I felt the nervous twinge, thinking someone might pull me aside and have me explain myself. No one has, because technically, I am not breaking the *three-one-one rule*. You know the rule. It's the one that allows you to take all of your favorite liquids with you from city to city as you make your way through the airports. Up to three (3) ounces of your shampoo, conditioner, and God-knows-what-else you might want to bring in one (1) quart bag per one (1) person – the 3-1-1 rule. I'm astonished that just a few ounces of shampoo is so critical to people. Don't they know the loved ones they're going to visit or the hotel they are registered at will gladly supply them with some? Why not be practical like me? My one quart bag holds nine, 50mL bottles of bourbon. Why spend $7-12 per drink at the airport for one drink, when one can slip into the bathroom and chug one down on the cheap? Right?! *Has everyone lost their minds?* I wonder.

After a quick stop in the bathroom to pour two mini-bottles into the cup of ice I just waited ten minutes in line for at the coffee stand, I make my way to the Mexican restaurant/bar for a quick bite before my flight. The burrito I have ordered is probably the worst thing I have tasted in a long time. I remember thinking, *I'm not sure what is in this thing, but how they get away with calling them eggs, I'll never know.* At least the whiskey I ordered is tolerable. I have ordered a double on the rocks and yes, my "coffee" cup is also there for me to sip on. I have sent the burrito back and decided against breakfast, however, the server insists on bringing me another.

Meanwhile, a very attractive woman has made her way close to me, and we start some small talk. Mutual travelers can usually find something in common to chat about for a couple of minutes, but this woman really speaks my language. It turns out she is looking forward to a pre-flight cocktail and is looking for something a little exotic. I just happen to have an app on my phone for such an occasion. After having the bartender follow the recipe we agreed upon from my phone app, my mutual traveler and I are chatting like old friends.

The waitress brought me another burrito and I decided to try again. One bite in, I am still not impressed with my breakfast. I ask that it be removed. Halfway through this fantastically yummy, blue rum concoction the bartender has created, my new friend, who is overtly flirting with me, begins to speak in a language that is completely incomprehensible. I have no idea what she is saying. My body became instantly drenched with sweat, as if someone has dumped a bucket of water on me. My internal voice (you know the one) is screaming at me, "*What is going on? What is she saying?*" I am now acutely aware that I am in pain. My midsection is on fire and great pressure is settling in. The sudden onset and the intensity of pain I am currently experiencing is almost incomprehensible. I wonder if I've been shot and just hadn't heard the gunfire, but I'm in an airport, so that *couldn't* be the case...*could it?*

As I scramble internally to understand what she is talking about, I notice the look of complete concern on her face. She has motioned to the bartender, who is also displaying concern as he looks at me. I think I make sense as I excuse myself. I need to get to my gate, so I can board this flight to San Francisco.

With a quick stop in the restroom, I look at my reflection in the mirror and it's not good. My coloring doesn't look good, I'm a sweaty mess, and my face is twisted from wincing at the pain radiating from my midsection. I feel compelled to get out of the airport and onto the plane. *The "show" must go on*, I tell myself. You see, there are only five of us seminar leaders who work for the company based in San Diego. It's not like just anyone could fill in or the 50+ people scheduled to be at the presentation tomorrow could just be left hanging. I HAD to get there.

So, barely able to stand or walk, I make it to the gate, to find I will be delayed for three hours due to a mechanical situation with the plane. *What to do?* I know I cannot leave my assistant sitting at the airport in San Francisco. I have to get there not just for him, but for my job. I have presentations in 4 cities this week. *I'm finally making money and have a plan for the future. I cannot lose this income now.* I am hoping this feeling will pass, but it is becoming rapidly apparent that I may need medical attention.

9:45 AM

Hunched over in a horrifically uncomfortable plastic chair at the gate, a feeling is coming over me I have not felt in 15 years (more on that in a moment). The heat I felt from my midsection has dispersed and I am hot all over. The real concern at this point is the growing pain in my upper abdominal area. With every breath, the pain is intensifying and I really don't know how much more of this I can take. In addition to the pain, there is that odd feeling nagging me, which I mentioned I hadn't felt in over a decade: I am going to be sick. I get up and walk to the rest room, located two gates down. It is a painful walk, but I am excited, thinking if I get sick and get rid of the breakfast burrito that was obviously *no good*, I will begin to feel much better. I make it to a stall and vomit. I have not done that in years. Purging the burrito, I believe I am on the road to recovery.

Walking back to my gate, I stop to purchase a sports drink. Everyone knows electrolytes and fluids after a long night/day of drinking will cure anything, right? I make it back to my plastic chair at the gate and settle in for what should be a tolerable wait for my delayed flight.

I become acutely aware that some of the other travelers can actually see the scythe in the hand of Death, as he hovers next to me. I envision death from an episode of *Family Guy*, better yet, maybe he is attractive like Brad Pitt's character in *Meet Joe Black*. Either way, I began to really believe I was dying. I had been battling negative and even suicidal thoughts over the last few years, but this was different. I can't really explain it other than there was an acceptance somewhere in my mind that I really *was* dying. What made me so sure the people at the airport knew I was in trouble was the fact that a random stranger, an elderly woman, approached me, extended her hand toward me, and asked me to take the pills in her hand. Looking in her hand, I did not have the choice of a red or blue pill as in *The Matrix* or *Alice in Wonderland*, but now I was sure I had slipped into the rabbit hole, and climbing my way out at this point was not an option.

> I become aware other travelers can see Death as he hovers next to me.

This is what I already knew: getting a person, especially one you do not know, to cross a room for you is not the easiest thing to do. I know, because I have only been compelled to do it a couple of times in my life. So, here I am, a nice woman extending two pills to me and asking as kind as can be, if I will take them. I let her know I don't take pills. You should know, because I am a heavy drinker, I won't take pills. I am concerned about the harm they may cause to my liver…you know, the one I batter daily with huge amounts of alcohol. Heaven forbid I damage my liver or kidneys by taking a couple of pills! She says to me, *she would feel a lot better, if I would take them.* I look around (for the hidden camera) and notice many of the people sitting near me want me to take the pills. She says they are for pain. God knows I am in pain, so I swallow them down with a big chug from my electrolyte sports drink.

11:00 AM

Over an hour and a half has passed and the pain in my midsection is nearly intolerable. I know I am in trouble and in need of medical attention. I also know the show must go on. I must make this flight. I believe I have to have an "industrial-sized" case of food poisoning. *Damn burrito!* I shift my weight in my chair every 20-30 seconds, looking for relief. It does not come. I like to believe I have a high tolerance for pain, but this has gotten ridiculous. I know not to ask the gate agent nearby for help, as this will ensure I will not make the flight. I gather myself and ask the person next to me to keep an eye on my bags. Breaking airport protocol, I leave my belongings with a stranger and walk three gates down.

Just standing up and making my way to the agent proves to be difficult...almost more than I can bare. As I think about how to phrase my question for the agent so she won't be obligated to call for medical help right then and there, I ask her what the process might be if someone thought they needed immediate medical attention. She let me know that paramedics would be called to check a person out. If this "hypothetical person" I was asking about was truly in dire straits, they would be carted off for a more intensive examination. *I would surely miss my flight. I would be taken to a local hospital.* I just knew it. I couldn't do that to myself, my assistant, the company I worked for, or the attendees that were scheduled to be at my meeting the next day. A little disappointed but definitely not surprised, I thanked her and let her know I would keep it under advisement. I turn and make my way back to my things. As I tried to settle back into the plastic seat, the constant shifting and growing pain continues. I call my assistant to let him know about the delay and to map out a route to the closest emergency department to the hotel convention center we will be staying at. Not to worry him too much, I let him know about the horrible burrito that is causing me such problems.

I call my office and speak to the coordinator to inform her I am not feeling well. I will make it to my destination, but if I am not feeling better, I am not sure how I will be able to conduct a seminar. This is strange for me to even think (let alone say) I may not be able to perform. For more than seven years combined, I had conducted these seminars. Now still relatively "new" with my second stint with the company, I had only ever missed one meeting. I missed that class due to an unintentional grounding of a plane I was on, preventing me from making it to my destination. I am truly in uncharted waters here.

After that call, I phoned another seminar leader who lives in the San Francisco area. She was coming to watch me to pick up a few pointers. I informed her to be ready, as I am not feeling well and not sure if I can do it. This would be a huge financial opportunity for her, while at the same time, costing me a lot of money. (Oh…and by the way, the *unintentional grounding* I just mentioned…that was MY doing. I caused a plane to land in Albuquerque, New Mexico. I never told anyone until now…it was a panic attack, and I had to get off of that plane. That's a story for another day.)

12:15 PM

It's now been nearly three hours of pain that gets worse every couple of minutes, and much like that *equation* I was working on during my car accident all those years ago, I again find myself *doing math*. Whoever said there would never be a need for algebra after high school was dead wrong. If I can just make it another half hour, my flight will begin boarding. At that point, I will arrive in San Francisco in a couple of hours. So, I'm thinking in two hours, I will have access to medical care. I can do this. It won't be easy, but it is manageable. Not only is the pain in my midsection and chest (yes, it is spreading) nearly impossible to describe at this point, but I notice my breathing has become labored too. I am trying to breathe in a manner that does not hurt. I must be quite the sight – sweating, adjusting in my seat, breathing is becoming more and more sporadic, color draining from my face.

I am approached by a second stranger, this time a man. He lets me know his wife (an entirely different lady than before) would like me to take a couple of pain pills. He has them in his outstretched hand. This time, there is no argument, nor internal conflict. I will take anything, so long as the pain is diminished.

At that time, I hear my name being paged on the overhead intercom. My brain instantly runs to the negative. I consider myself a positive person, but in this moment, all I can come up with is they are not going to allow me to get on the plane. I just keep thinking, *why am I being called out? Am I going to be denied access to my flight? Did I sit here in pain for hours just to be denied boarding?*

I approach the gate agent, even though I have done everything in my power to avoid her up 'til now. She smiles and informs me I have been upgraded to first class. This was a little unexpected and very welcomed, as I usually receive this upgrade before reaching the airport. I have flown first class too many times to count, and as great as the extra room is for my tall frame, it is the free booze that I really enjoy. Today, I know I will not be ordering anything to drink. I just need to make it to San Francisco.

12:45 PM

Pre-boarding has begun, and the agent has just announced first class may now begin boarding. Usually, I am one of the first in line. I want to make sure there is room for my carry-on in the overhead bin and I want to stretch out with a glass of bourbon in hand, regardless of the hour of day. Not so today. I am elated to have made it to boarding – a true testament to my determination to make it to my destination. *Things should go smoothly from here*, I think to myself.

I slowly make my way up to the jet-way and walk toward the plane. I look at my ticket and see I am seated in 1C, first row – aisle. I round the corner as I step onto the plane and I see my seatmate for the first time. By the look of excitement, the smile on her face and the drink in hand, I quickly determine this is her first time travelling in first class. As she makes eye contact with me, her smile quickly disappears. The excitement that I saw in her eyes, just a few seconds ago, has been replaced with horror. She sees something in (or around) me that I am not even aware of.

As a seminar leader, one gets really good at reading body language and facial expressions. Yes, it's definitely horror she is projecting. I instantly begin wondering what it is she sees. Is it the animated Death character from *The Family Guy* or *Meet Joe Black*, others seemed to see earlier? I feel bad for her, as what was once going to be a fun experience for her has now turned into *death watch*. It's not just my seatmate, but also the attendant in first class who looks at me with fear in her eyes.

The attendant wants to know if I am feeling alright. Is there anything she can get for me? Am I comfortable? I let her know I am fine and just want to make it through this short flight. A short flight, indeed – it should be just an hour and a half to San Francisco. My mind is working in overdrive, coming up with all sorts of equations and scenarios as to how I will make it. *It is 1.5 hours to SF, which is really only an hour of flight time, with the last half hour being the descent.* Do you ever do things like that, and break them down into more manageable parts? I do that all the time, and in this moment, I thought it was working for me.

It is settled: I just need to hold it together for an hour, and then I can focus on the descent and landing. My seatmate is keeping an eye on me the whole time, like one of those reptiles that can move its eyes independently of one another. I can feel it. I am wondering if (and secretly hoping) she works in the medical field, but don't want to find out the answer is truly "yes," so I ignore the inquisitive eye. Just 45 minutes into the flight (the true half-way point and only 15 minutes until the beginning of our descent), I am going to be sick again. Until today, I have not vomited in more than 15 years, and now at more than 30,000 feet, I am about to be sick for the second time today.

1:30 PM (37,000 feet – somewhere between PHX and SFO)

I am very grateful there are no cameras in this tiny restroom onboard. *Seriously, how could there even be room for one to stand in here, let alone get down on all fours?,* I thought. I think about how hard one would be laughing to watch someone my size contort his body to make sure what he was expelling was making it into the toilet. This was no small feat. Obviously, I have known for hours now that I am in need of medical attention. Now, I have no doubt. There is blood in my vomit. *What was in that burrito anyway!?* I am cracking jokes in my head, but reality is taking over.

Something internally is greatly wrong and the pain that has now spread from a small area in my midsection to include my entire torso. Because of the pain between my neck and waist, I am convinced I am experiencing a heart attack. *What else could this possibly be?* The "good news" is that our descent should begin any minute.

Upon exiting the tiny onboard restroom, I finally acknowledge to the flight attendant I am not feeling well. I ask if she can call the gate and have a wheelchair meet us at the gate. The thought of trying to walk all the way to baggage claim and the car rental area is unbearable. She lets me know having a wheelchair meet me at the gate is only possible under one condition, because I did not have one to board the plane. If I truly want one, I would be met by paramedics, as well. They would have to check me out, before letting anyone else deplane. As someone who knows how wasteful time can be at airports, I decide I could not do that to the other 160 passengers on board.

> I must be having a heart attack. What else could this possibly be?

I inform her I will tough it out. After much tossing and turning in my seat, we finally land. I know help is not far away. I call my assistant from the runway to find out where he will pick me up. He hasn't even picked up the rental car yet. He's been chilling at a restaurant still inside the airport. *What!?* I tell him to get the car as soon as possible and I will meet him at the rental area as quickly as I could.

2:30 PM (SFO)

Now five hours into the worst airport travelling experience of my life, it takes everything I have just to make it to my feet, grab my carryon bags, and exit the plane. The slight, uphill angle of the jetway was incredibly difficult to walk up. I think to myself, *I might as well be walking up one of the steep roadways San Francisco is known for, but this is just the 30 feet to get inside the airport. How am I ever going to make it?* I am so weak, I'm barely able to pull my roller-board behind me, even though it's on wheels. With pressure bearing down on my chest and my labored breathing, my suitcase feels as though it weighs 300 pounds. I am walking so slowly, young children are passing me by as if I am standing still.

After what seems like an eternity on the slow-moving passenger tram from Terminal 5 to the car rental pickup at San Francisco International, I finally round the corner to the car company with which I have my rental reservation. I am completely dismayed to see a line of at least 30 people. There is my assistant at the halfway point. *Unacceptable!!!* I cannot wait any longer. I need to get to the hospital. I am finally ready to admit to myself I am experiencing a true medical emergency. I notice three kiosks that no one is using. Everyone is standing in line to deal with an agent. As a seasoned traveler, I utilize kiosks as much as possible. I bypass everyone and check-in quickly at the machine. It only takes 3-4 minutes, and I have my rental agreement in hand. I motion to my assistant to get out of that ridiculously long line and meet me at the car pick up area.

We get in the car and he wants to know just what has happened to me. We had spoken just hours before and I was upbeat, looking forward to a great week. Sure, I had mentioned the burrito, but we both knew that could not be responsible for this. I now sat slouched over in the passenger seat next to him. At this point, seminar be damned, I just need to make sure my assistant is taken care of for the night, before taking me to the emergency department. As someone who worked in a hospital through college, I knew once we made it to the hospital, I would be there for a good amount of time, and possibly overnight. We arrive at the hotel, I slap down my credit card and get checked in to our rooms. Without ever making it to the rooms, I hand a key to my assistant and tell him, "Now, get me to a hospital."

Although the hospital was just 15 minutes away, it felt like it was taking hours to get there. First, trying to get to the hospital was difficult, because we both had our phone navigations set to the same destination, but both of the automated voices were giving different directions. It was frustrating to be talking over both of them, as I tried to explain how I was feeling. Secondly, he wanted to tell me why I was feeling the way I was. *Really?!* He had no idea what I went through to get to San Francisco or the crushing pain I was in. *Obviously, this is simply the worst case of food poisoning ever...right?* He just kept talking and talking and talking. I was growing more and more irritated.

Finally, the hospital was in sight. As we entered the parking area, I pointed to the ambulance bay. I knew not to be dropped off there, however, the main entrance had to be close by. Sure enough, we found the doors I was looking for and I instructed him to let me out, before he looked for a parking space. Feeling completely exhausted and relieved as I limp into the hospital, I walk right past the check-in area and head straight for the double doors leading to the emergency room. I pushed the doors as hard as I could and was thrilled they opened.

The nurses in the emergency room looked at me like I was breaking into the place, and in fairness...I was. I had just broke protocol and had not checked in at the front desk. There was no handing over insurance cards, verifying coverage, or talking to anyone in reception. I needed help and I needed it now. I was a little relieved to see the general layout of this

> I needed help, and I needed it now!

emergency room was similar to the one where I worked. I saw the "cardiac triage" area and made a direct path for it. Now that I was actually on hospital grounds, I allowed myself to think about what may actually be wrong with me other than food poisoning. The only thing I was coming up with was my heart. As I used the last little bit of energy I had left, I laid down on the cart and hoped someone would be in to find me...before I died.

3:45 PM (Emergency Department)

Two nurses quickly attach leads to my chest, the monitor is beeping and I know I will be taken care of. I give the quick recap of the meal that led to all of this, still hoping for it to be food poisoning, but knowing better. One nurse asks me if I have been drinking today. "Of course not," I reply. And truthfully, on any other afternoon, I would have had several glasses on the plane and while in the car to the hotel. Today however, was not like any other day. I have completely forgotten about all of the bourbon and rum in Phoenix I'd had between 8:00 am and 9:30 am. That didn't really "count" as today anyway...that was early this morning. Besides, as much as I drink and with my tolerance for alcohol, that is clearly not the problem here.

After 15-20 minutes of extremely close monitoring, it is determined that I *do* have an irregular heartbeat, but I am *not* having a heart attack. I am moved to another examination area. Another nurse is getting me situated and hooked up to the monitors in this area. Blood is being drawn, oxygen tubing is placed in my nose and the question is asked again: "How much have you had to drink today?" "Nothing today," I let her know. Again, I am not intentionally lying, I am unaware of just how bad things have gotten and not really grasping the severity of what has happened over the last few hours.

My mind is struggling to keep up with how I got *here* – not just the emergency room in San Francisco, 750 miles away from where my day started, but *here* as in...life. As my body and internal organs start shutting down, the details seem less and less important.

During the next 25 minutes filled with nurses and technicians coming in and out of the trauma unit, I try to keep calm. I know I'm dying. Deep down, I've actually known it for quite some time now.

It's not even the first time in my life that I've known Death has come for me. *"I'm still not ready to go,"* I think to myself, but the thought of accepting this fate and having all the pain leave me seems pretty tempting. I wonder to myself if anyone would really miss me if I died right here, right now. These dark thoughts and almost accepting this fate were put on hold, momentarily. Lab test results began coming in, and they were not good. The results showed my internal organs were, in fact, shutting down. The emergency room staff, working diligently to keep me alive, were stunned to see this much damage done to someone not even 40 years old.

"I believe you are in this position due to alcohol," the doctor says. Again, I let them know *I haven't been drinking*. But, in that moment, I realize today wasn't the problem. Today was just the last straw. I've been drinking non-stop for nearly 25 years. For the first time in more than a decade, it's time to have an honest conversation about my drinking.

The doctor uses the word "alcoholism" several times as he talks to me. The word seems to hang in the air before hitting me right between the eyes each time he says it.

> *Alcoholism?!? This has got to be a mistake. Sure, I might drink a lot and I've known deep down it's too much. Heck, I even know I've been sick for quite some time, but alcoholism?! I'm NOT an alcoholic! I'm not!!*

More tests confirm my pancreas is dying, my liver and kidneys are severely damaged, and my body is filled with a bacteria called *C. difficile* (a killer of 30,000 per year in the US). This bacteria infects the intestines, causing some pretty disgusting symptoms, and come to find out, it's actually raging throughout my *entire* body. The reality that all of this was happening due to my drinking was completely overwhelming.

In this moment, I didn't want to believe it. I didn't want to even think about it. All I really wanted was something for the pain. I was letting them poke and prod at me. They were running their tests. They had still not given me anything for the pain. Now, he wants to talk to me about my drinking?! Still somewhat defiant, I let him know I need something for the pain. I will tell him *anything* – even the truth about how much I drink and how often, if he'd just give me something. A few short minutes later, they put some morphine in my IV bag and the pain is instantly...tolerable. It was not gone, but at least it was lessened a bit. *Finally!!!*

It wasn't supposed to happen this way. I had a plan...a good one at that. I had planned to QUIT drinking on my 40th birthday. I wanted to show people we can quit whatever we want, whenever we want. This plan to keep this absurd amount of drinking up until my 40th birthday was a big part of my vision to build an online community at ifinallyquit.com, although (at the time) not in existence yet. I had been able to hide my excessive drinking from so many people for so long, and it was pretty scary to think it had caught up with me. When I say *caught up with me*, it would still take many more days for my brain to catch up with what was actually happening here. Had I not made it to the emergency room when I did, or if I'd been left untreated for just a few more minutes, I most definitely would have died.

> **It wasn't supposed to happen this way...I had a plan...**

Minute by minute, hospital staff fought to keep me alive the first few days. Actually, I would not leave the hospital for fourteen days, eight days of which I spent in the Intensive Care Unit. The ICU is by far the last place a person or any medical staff wants a patient to be. The hospital employees as a whole do everything in their power to get a person out of the ICU as quickly as possible, due to the cost of keeping them there. The more time that went by, the more I thought things like, *how much money is this stay costing me and my insurance company? How much damage had I done? If my body is truly falling apart, how have I been able to function for so long?* It was time to face reality, but reality would have to wait a few more days. Right here, right now, it was going to take all of my effort just to stay alive...

I would lay in the ICU for more than a week, and for three of those days I was kept in a medically-induced coma, feeling scared and embarrassed. I soon came to realize what a blessing this time really was. With each passing day, I was facing the reality that I had been dying. My internal organs were in turmoil and the negative thoughts of my mind were racing. Fear, shame, and self-doubt were running rampant in my mind. *Would I be able to hold on to this second chance?* I wondered. Or, *was it really more like the fifth or sixth chance?*

Could I use this dying experience to motivate myself to change? Or better yet, could I motivate and encourage others? Yes, that is what I'd do, I'd show others that change and quitting are possible. But where to begin? To understand how I got to this place in life, I want to take you back and look at what I had done with my life the last few years. This type of mental and physical damage had been building for a very long time. For me to explain to you how I ended up in the ICU in 2011, let me take you back to where most of this began just six short years before...

3

Somebody to Love

2005 (La Jolla, CA)

Six years before I would fight for my life in the ICU of San Francisco, I was living in a pretty affluent area of San Diego called La Jolla. Life was good. Not only did I have a great apartment within walking distance of bars and restaurants I liked to frequent, but I had a few friends in the area, too. On the weekends, we'd usually start at my apartment for "pre" happy hour cocktails and catch up with what transpired in each other's lives during the previous week. After a few drinks, cigarettes, and story-telling, we'd head out for the evening. I was accustomed to (and enjoyed) covering the bar tab at the end of the night. For me, it wasn't just the weekends when I got to enjoy what La Jolla had to offer, but because of my *work* schedule, I was also able to visit a lot of bars throughout the week.

I was working for a company that scheduled, promoted, booked, and conducted seminars throughout the United States for the medical and dental community. As a seminar leader, my schedule was such that I really only worked about 28 weeks out of the year. Sure, I was in a different city every day and the travel was grueling, but when I was home, there was no office to go into or clock to punch. I had plenty of money and tons of time. I really had no complaints or wants for anything. Well, maybe there were times when I was a little lonely or thought about how it would be to have a "significant other" in my life, but that hadn't happened for me yet.

One fateful weekend, one of my married friends had signed us up for a party bus that was making a few stops at apartment complexes in our area then dropping the group off in downtown San Diego – the Gaslamp District. We were hooked immediately. There were 50 bars and restaurants to visit on any given night, not just the three or four we'd grown accustomed to in La Jolla. The Gaslamp area had everything: ethnic food, sports bars, dance clubs…everything.

Within a short amount of time, I found my dream condo just outside of the Gaslamp District. I was so close to the action – I loved it. I could walk out to the bars and stumble home every night while in San Diego. On the weekends, the "crew" would pack bags for the weekend and stay at my place – less than 15 miles from their homes. It was a little lazy, but at least no one was going to get a DUI this way.

We were having the time of our lives. For me, I wasn't just going out on the weekends, but it was truly an every night occasion. I was able to find seven or eight bars that I really enjoyed and quickly became a regular whenever I was not travelling. Being a regular had its advantages at many of these bars, like the manager comping me a free drink or two during the week, because I had run up such big tabs on the weekends. Although financially not necessary, free drinks just seemed to taste a little bit better, so I always appreciated them when they'd show up.

After several months of this schedule — flying in and out of San Diego every other week and partying it up with my friends on the weekends — we all decided to take a weekend off from the

Gaslamp and go out in La Jolla for *old time's sake*.

That's when it happened...out of the blue, one of my friends I'd not seen in about six months walked into the bar with a tall, gorgeous, new-to-town client of his. She carried herself incredibly well, and by the end of the evening, we'd decided to go on a date. She was a nurse working 12 hour shifts, so between the two of our schedules the first available day we could go out happened to be on Valentine's Day.

Little did I know this was the beginning of what would seem like a fairy tale...yes, some of us men look for that, too. I flew out of town for work and had a very profitable week. This time the anticipation of getting back home to San Diego was overwhelming. It had been months if not years since I looked forward to a date this much.

We got together and of course headed right out to the Gaslamp, making my usual stops where everyone knew my name. The personal attention and treatment I received from the bartenders, managers, and owners of the places we went was through the roof. I think they were as excited for me as I was to be on a date with someone so suited to me. I stand tall at 6'-6" and she was fit and 6'-1". Her smile lit up any dark bar we visited. Our height and excellent "pairing" if you will was noticed by everyone. We definitely stood out in a crowd. And, to add to our compatibility, we both drank and smoked, although the amounts were totally different.

During our first date, while we were outside one of the bars smoking, a homeless man approached me and asked how tall I was. Being asked how tall I am was something I was very used to. That question is usually followed with another..."Did you ever play basketball?" His follow up question was different. He asked, "Don't you find it difficult to find shoes?" I did, actually. Wearing a size 15 makes it fairly difficult to just find something off the shelf.

I understood instantly why, as a man living on the street, who stood nearly tall enough to look me in the eye, would ask such a question. I looked down to see extremely battered shoes and he began to show me the holes in the bottom. I could see where his train of thought was going, so I cut him off mid-sentence and asked if he could meet me at this exact spot at 10:00 am the next morning. I told him I'd bring him some shoes and asked if there was anything else I could bring him. The next morning, sure enough, he was there and I left him with shoes, socks, pants, and a few bucks.

What a catch I must have seemed at the time to my date. Everywhere we went people knew me and spoke highly of me, I spent money as if I could print more at my condo overnight, and she just watched me commit to give another human what he needed without any thought or care about it. For the most part, I was good-natured and had a deep desire to please and take care of others. I genuinely did (and do) want the best for everyone. However, I did have one major flaw she wouldn't find out about for weeks later…at my core…I was a drunk. She had no idea what she was really in for or who I really was. Heck, at the time…*I* didn't even know.

> At my core, I was a drunk. She had no idea what she was in for.

We continued seeing each other every opportunity when I was in San Diego and she wasn't working. She'd come pick me up from whatever bar or situation I'd gotten myself into and I could tell after just a few weeks, she was growing weary of my lifestyle. So…I did what anyone completely out of touch with reality would do…I asked her to marry me. She didn't say yes right away, so over the next couple of weeks, I was relentless in my pursuit of her. She finally agreed to marry me.

When she said yes, something crazy happened (at least crazy to me). As if a "switch" had been flipped somewhere in her head, she let me know exactly how this marriage was going to go down. You see, I didn't realize that nearly all women from about the age of eight have made up their mind as to how they want to get married. The wedding had to be perfect.

She let me know she was going to be in the best shape of her life, we'd get married on the beach in the Florida Keys with sand in our toes, her hair would be the longest it had ever been, and we would drink Mai Thais. I was amazed at the detail she had considered. She described everything…all the way down to the car ride to the upcoming nuptial event. I, on the other hand, was just thankful that someone as beautiful and good-natured as her wanted to be with me.

Unlike her, I was not making any such statements or commitments. As long as I didn't have to change my actions and behaviors, I was all good. I continued to smoke a pack or two a day and drink hard alcohol as if it would be taken away and wiped off the surface of the planet the very next day. What happened over the next six months was the beginning of my demise. I'd held together my overindulgence for over a decade, so I didn't see this coming at all.

I watched this already beautiful woman transform her body and mind…all in her commitment to herself and me, but I didn't see it that way at the time. It's funny to think back and realize I was watching this whole thing, but I didn't *see*. It would actually take me years to fully understand what had been standing right in front of me.

She said she would be fit and in the best shape of her life, and one way she planned to do that was to cycle. She purchased a mountain bike AND a road bike, spending thousands of dollars. One day, she informed me she enrolled in a 100 mile bike ride! *100 miles – Really?!* She began to run a few days a week as well, which turned into ultimately running in the San Diego Rock 'n' Roll Marathon. As one who never understood this level of exercise, I was blown away at the amount of time, energy, and expense a person could put into working out. I did my best to be part of what she was doing. However, in hindsight, all I can do now is shake my head at my absurdity and level at which I allowed alcohol to lead me and my decisions.

During her first 100 mile bike ride, I drove her and the bike to the event only because there happened to be a casino with a bar nearby. Doing some quick research on the internet and quizzing my fiancé ever so slightly, I figured it would take six or seven hours for her to complete her ride. This let me know exactly how many cocktails I could consume and still make it back to the finish line (me and my math again…). Before your mind starts to wander off and think I didn't make the finish line, let me tell you I was *always* at the finish line. But, just because I was physically there, didn't always mean I should have been.

I was so proud of her as she completed this 100 mile bike ride, but had no concept of what her body had just been through. We made it home without incident after her bike event, unlike when she completed the San Diego Marathon a few months later…

The day of her marathon, I dropped her off as close as possible to the starting/staging area. I don't recall the exact time, but I do know it was very, very early in the day. There were people EVERYWHERE, as the event draws about 30,000 participants. I had made up my mind I would not be driving to the finishing area to pick her up. We'd simply take a cab home so I wouldn't have to deal with the throng of people (the runners and their supporters), especially knowing I'd have some cocktails by then. In theory, this seemed like a great idea, but if you've ever seen the end of a race like this, you'd know it is bedlam and getting a cab would prove to be…challenging, to say the least.

Coincidentally, it took her about the same amount of time to run a marathon as it did to complete that long bike ride, so approximately six hours later, I found myself amongst a jovial group of people. Most of them had no desire to run 26+ miles, but definitely were there to cheer on a friend or loved one. It was a party – complete with booze and beer stands. *This marathon business wasn't so bad. Maybe, I had it all wrong*, I remember thinking.

Ooh, oh, there she is. Running with three other participants she'd met along the way, I could see her approaching the finish line. Again, I was so proud of her. As we found each other after she crossed the finish line, I could see she was elated. She wanted to take in every moment and to encourage and cheer on other runners as they approached the finish line. With a beer in her hand, I marveled at how lucky I truly was. As the runner's "high" began to wear off in the next hour, she was ready to get out of there. She asked if we could go and where I had parked. "Parked?" I said, "No, let's go get a cab."

We made our way to the exit and I was oblivious to the fact that with each further step, she was adding to an already 26+ mile day. Well, we couldn't find a cab, and in my determination, we walked over a mile just to get to a trolley station. Grabbing the trolley, we arrived at the stop outside of our building downtown just a couple of minutes later. Sitting caused her legs, body, and mind to accept what she had just done. Because the muscles in her legs were fatigued and cramping, it made it difficult for her to get off the trolley. She was exhausted.

Ultimately, we made it upstairs. After getting cleaned up and what I could only imagine had to be one of the best shower experiences of her life, she emerged from the bathroom…ready for bed. I couldn't allow that. I was too proud of her and wanted to *show off* my fiancé and tell others about her accomplishment. Since it was only about four in the afternoon, and time for *happy hour*, I convinced her to come out with me and have a beer or two so she could "carb up" after her grueling day.

> **Booze dictated my schedule nearly every day of my life.**

Booze really did dictate my schedule that day and quite frankly, nearly every day of my life. As we went from bar to bar that afternoon, she must have walked an additional five or six miles, before finally letting me know she just couldn't go on. I remember being disappointed. Can you believe that? I was disappointed I'd have to go home before happy hour was over. Well, we made it home and I took care of her, ordering in dinner and making sure she was comfortable. I didn't know the physical pain and the mental exhaustion a person has after a marathon, but in hindsight, dealing with me on a daily basis must have been five times more exhausting than any race ever could have been.

4

She's Gone

2006 (Downtown San Diego, CA)

I will now explain to you how I ultimately put my commitment to cigarettes and alcohol before everyone else. Part of the transformation my fiancé was going through included joining a gym. While working 12 hour shifts for three to four days a week, plus running and biking, she never complained about all the exercise she was putting in. She just simply wanted to be healthy, so she would be available to me for decades to come.

It must have been exasperating as she watched me not budge an inch in changing my routine of smoking, drinking, and being lazy while home, then flying back out of San Diego for weeks at a time. She was committed to our future, being in shape, and spending as much time together as possible...and I wasn't. She suggested I ride one of the bikes as she ran alongside, but I wasn't about to do that. I was content to be who I was, but I did know one thing...I wanted to be around her more than ever. I just wasn't willing to change *my* physical routine.

On a whim, I quit my job of four years as a seminar speaker. And yes, there was a lot of alcohol involved in the actual decision. I was convinced I could start my own business and we would live happily ever after. After all, this travel and being gone for a couple of weeks a month was great when single, but now I wanted to be home with her. I wish I could tell you that it was a fairy tale ending and that we lived happily ever after, but my drinking would catch up with me. Five years later I'd end up in an ICU fighting for my life…alone.

What really happened was I struggled tremendously to get my new business off of the ground. I went through my savings and ran up credit card debt like I'd never experienced before in life. We were living together by then, and just paying my half of the rent was nearly impossible. I was no longer the one supplying for everyone else. My married friends still came down and stayed over for weekends of drunkenness, although I couldn't foot the bill in the same manner in which I used to. I tried though, and I spent money I didn't have on booze. My friends had no idea at the time I was spending money I didn't have. I felt it necessary to keep up appearances. For the first time in my life, I was drinking more alcohol than I could afford, and still no warning bells were going off in my head. Actually, I began to drink more than ever before. A new, more vicious cycle started; one in which I wouldn't emerge from for nearly five years.

I came to the realization that I no longer had the money or the credit to sustain my lifestyle in downtown San Diego. I was also feeling as if I no longer "deserved" a woman of her caliber and beauty. I began to make changes in my behavior that would ultimately cause her to walk away from me. Never wanting to be the one to end things with her by just saying so or having an adult conversation about where I was in life, I became distant and mean. I took my drinking to a whole new level, even to the point when I completely embarrassed her by showing up as a patient at the emergency department where she was working at the time. I couldn't sleep that night, not because my mind was busy obsessing about the small details of something I just couldn't let go of or about wedding plans, but due to pain in my midsection.

That night in the emergency room should have been a glimpse into the future, but I didn't see the path I was on. One of the doctors gave me a speech about drinking to excess, the harm I could *potentially* do to myself, and how I should want to be healthy enough to keep this woman in my life. But my shame and embarrassment was not going to let that happen. In my mind, this engagement was already over. It wouldn't be long before the disengagement in my mind manifested in my physical world.

> She was gone, a blow that would take me years to overcome.

Just a few months later, she was gone. I sat alone in my condo not being able to make the monthly payments anymore. My drinking to excess had just cost me my engagement. As this story plays out, I would pay many more tangible and financial costs, but ending the engagement and completely separating from her was a blow that would take me years to overcome.

At the time of my disengagement, I had no job, no car, no money, and with the recent market collapse, I had no job prospects either. It turned out my particular skill set didn't lend itself well to a corporate nine to five type of job. As I began to beg, borrow, and make promises, life for me at this point had done a complete 180. I didn't know at the time that I wouldn't be able to fulfill my promises until six years later. And, although I had allowed my life to go this wrong this fast, surprisingly there was still much, much further to descend.

5

Brother, Can You Spare a Dime?

Things began spiraling downward quickly from here. I spent the next few months living on people's couches and grabbing a *free* meal anywhere I could. One thing that didn't change, was my consistent need to put cigarettes and booze before everything else. Somehow I was still allowing those inanimate objects to run my life and they were certainly in charge. At the end of this three-month period, one of my friends whose house I was staying in let me know it really wasn't acceptable to be sleeping on her couch with no end in sight. Something had to change and she let me know I'd outstayed my welcome. I had run out of places to stay in Southern California, and would have to begin looking for other places to go.

August 2006 (Fort Wayne, Indiana)

I finally made the embarrassing call to my brother back in Indiana. I let him know I really had nowhere to go and no money to my name. Like a true family member, he opened his home to me. Although he and his wife had only been married about a year, they found themselves with an unwanted house guest who had no plan. What a way to bring the "honeymoon phase" of their marriage to a screeching halt.

I didn't fit in there and really made little to no effort to do so. I was content to spend my days and nights in their basement, tucked away from them and society as a whole, camping out with my *demons*. As someone who obsesses over the smallest of details, I was having difficulty grasping the obvious things or at least figuring out what to do about them. Here I was... without a job and relying on my younger brother for assistance to make it through life. I sat in the basement every night consuming what I thought at the time was a disgusting amount of alcohol. Little did I know I'd make a promise to myself to drink even more...maxing out at a fifth of bourbon a day – that's the equivalent of nearly three six-packs of beer or four bottles of wine...a day! But, that was still a couple of years away. (Yes, I would commit to drinking even more, and somewhere in my mind, this made sense.)

I knew what I had already lost due to my consumption, but didn't know I still had more things to lose. What else could there have been? Just to recap, as I often did (I'd obsess relentlessly about my situation), I'd lost a six-figure annual income while really only working half of the year, friends and a fiancé, and perfect weather in San Diego, and replaced all of that with a very low-income, entry level position in Indiana. In fact, I was making so little money that my weekly food allowance was $10 per week. I would buy one jar of spaghetti sauce, a bag of frozen veggie "meat," and a box of noodles, and make that meager sustenance last a week at a time.

On my extremely limited income, I still made sure bourbon and cigarettes were always within my reach. I was spending more on cigarettes and whiskey every week than on food. I never expected to be this limited on funds for this long. It had been months now, and I still had not rebounded from losing it all in California. *Seriously, me of all people*, I would think to myself. *How do I make this end?* This limited food budget lasted far longer than I anticipated and I'd began to lose weight. I was too drunk to notice the weight coming off, but it was definitely something others around me noticed.

The tension that my level of drinking, smoking, and lack of income put on my brother and his newlywed was palpable, especially with my brother's desire to finally spend time with his "big" brother. As it turns out, my brother is a great man – caring for everyone around him. There were so many things I missed out on in his life due to my addiction to alcohol. Even in my teenage years, I drank to the point I would miss his Little League games and other important events. I should have been there for him. It was no wonder that, now that I was there and so dependent on him, he was willing to do anything to *please* his big brother.

They had a newborn on the way, too (*did I mention that?*), and a grown drunk already crowding their living space. Although my brother never wanted to have the conversation with me, it had to come. Just over six months of living there, with no real advancement being made on my part, he had to let me know I would need to move on. There were no ill feelings at all…it was just reality. I wasn't making enough money to contribute to their household, let alone to sustain my own apartment, nor was I making any great strides in that direction.

I could see it from their perspective, but at the time, my perspective mattered more. I was happy to wallow in self-pity, drunkenness, and shame. The truth is that inside my mind, I was emotionally living in a place that allowed me to be the victim in everything. *It wasn't me,* I would tell myself, *it was the market – no one was making money.* But, the fact was, everyone else was paying their bills, driving their cars, going to work, and loving one another. I really did not know it at the time, but I had lost something, and I didn't even know what that *something* was. Sadly, the damage I'd left in my wake was done. Just a few months later, his marriage would end. I'm not taking full responsibility for it, but I'd be a fool not to realize I contributed to their demise.

The embarrassment and shame continued to grow, taking over parts of me that used to carry confidence, success, and empowerment. It was hard enough having my immediate family know how I was living. My pride certainly didn't allow me to let friends know where I was or how I was living. In reality, the time had come to make other arrangements again. But where would I go this time? I placed the phone call to my sister in Florida. It turned out, this first trip to her place would permanently alter the path of my life. It was the start of earning the nickname "the quitter," not because I would give up easily, but because even though I didn't know it at the time, I was about to get rid of a 20-year habit. In ditching this 20-year habit, I'd have an epiphany that would keep me up at night, until I could fill a void fueled by my compulsiveness.

> Embarrassment and shame took over where confidence and success used to be.

At this time, I'd been *homeless* for almost an entire year. I had no idea my drinking would cause me to slip even further, and it would be another three years until I would have my own place again. Until then, my "darkest" days would become even darker, and I would suffer with thoughts of suicide along with long bouts of depression. But, ultimately, my determination would cause a huge transformation. I had a fateful encounter coming with my 11-year-old niece that would change me forever.

6

Sweet Sister Mercy

June 2007

The embarrassment of my sister and niece picking me up at the airport in Tampa was almost more than I could bear. My sister's eyes welled up with tears when she saw the physical shape I was in. I didn't see what she saw…sure, I was a little thinner than usual, but I was still alright…so I thought. My $10 food budget along with my nearly $100 drinking allowance per week had made a noticeable change in my appearance. And, that wasn't $100 of the "good" stuff, rather I would search out the biggest bottles of the cheapest whiskey I could find.

I was malnourished and my internal organs (especially my liver) were swollen to the point my belly stuck out abruptly from just below my rib cage. Unlike my sister who was old enough to understand and be saddened by my appearance, my niece didn't know any better, and was just excited to have her uncle there. She was too young to understand this extended, open-ended visit was really a desperate attempt on my part to rejoin society. The truth was, I was homeless. Sure I wasn't sleeping on the streets or in parks every night, although there had been a couple of those nights. I was homeless in every sense of the word, and thank God I hadn't burned every bridge with friends and family…yet.

Moving to Florida happened four years prior to my perilous emergency room and ICU stay. While with my sister and her family, I continued to drink at an alarming rate, and thought I was hiding the actual amount from them. But, consuming a fifth of bourbon—17 glasses a day—really doesn't go unnoticed. Actually, a huge spotlight would be cast on me before I would be able to finally quit drinking, but not yet. Quitting didn't happen while I was in Florida. Before I'd give up the bottle for good, I had to figure out how to quit smoking first.

It turned out, the missing piece in quitting smoking for me would be compassion for my fellow man (or young lady, rather): my niece. She was actually the catalyst who influenced me to quit smoking. By the time I ended up at their home in Florida, it had been several years since I'd last seen or spent time with my sister and her daughter. Before showing up flat broke and literally nowhere else to go, I remember her being one of the happiest babies...ever. As an infant, toddler, and young child, her laugh was infectious. People noticed her laugh at all times. There was talk (within the family) of recording her laugh and sending it off to toy companies. That laughter, placed in the right toy, would make more money than all toys in the history of the world. Okay, maybe a bit of an exaggeration, but you get what I'm saying...her laughter was awesome. Flash forward back to the present, something had certainly changed for the worse.

This is going to be candid, so please do not judge, as if this is the only family on the planet, or in the United States, or in Florida, where the inhabitants smoke indoors. There is no blame...period. It is what it is – nothing more and nothing less. Like me, my sister and her husband had been life-long smokers. With them living in the Midwest and now Florida for the entirety of my niece's existence on this planet, she had lived her whole life engulfed in second-hand smoke. This wasn't bad parenting or anything like that. I also grew up in a house of second hand smoke. Many of you reading this book right now grew up in that type of environment or raised children while you smoked in the house, too. So again, I stress…there is no blame. This is simply the environment in which my niece had grown up – just like us.

For as long as I can remember, my mother and most of her family were smokers. I vividly remember spending time as a young boy at my grandparents' home in Garden Grove, California. My grandmother would be on the couch with her menthol cigarettes and my grandfather with his pipe, smoking like they did not have a care in the world. My mother always made sure she had a carton of menthols in the refrigerator, a pack in her cigarette case, and "emergency back-up packs" in her purse and glove compartment of the car.

At around ten years of age, some of my friends and I would occasionally steal a cigarette or two out of my mother's case. I learned early on that a true smoker has an incredibly accurate count of just how many cigarettes they have left throughout the house. *My math skills would be honed for this and booze later on in life.* Once my mother caught on, she had a sure-fire way of deterring me from smoking, or so she thought. As I stood in the backyard of our small apartment with my step-father, he gave me a speech about *being a man*. Now that I was *all grown up* (at the age of ten), he thought I should have my first cigar. Puffing on that big, green, gnarly thing, I wanted to prove I WAS A MAN now. I don't know how many shades of green I turned before I started puking, but I suppose I could have won an Olympic medal for projectile vomiting (had such an event existed). This stopped me from smoking for about five years.

After being uprooted from southern California in the mid-80's, I found myself as teenager in Indiana trying to fit in. During junior high, I started smoking. At first, it was not very often:

just one or two before school and a couple after school. Then it became *cool*. I'd hang out with the older kids, trying to sneak out of school during lunch to have a quick smoke. Had I got caught, there would have been dire consequences, well for a teenager that is. Getting caught implies doing something wrong, which meant having to face my mother, Saturday school, or detention. I knew I should quit, so I decided to. Unfortunately, my new-found habit already had a lock-tight grip on me…and I was just 15!

At the age of 16, I purchased my first smoking cessation aid. It was a plastic cigarette, designed to *feel* like a cigarette in the hand, and allow one to act like they were smoking. I puffed away on that thing for days, in between cigarettes, and thinking, *if I just cut down, I will be better off*. As my habit developed, I was smoking more and more.

Even back then, with the low cost of cigarettes (before they jacked the prices to cover the punitive damages from lawsuits for shortening people's lives and causing diseases, none of which means anything to a teenager), I told myself, *when a pack costs $2 I will quit*. A few years later, I had raised the cut-off price to $2.50 a pack. I thought about quitting smoking all the time: through college, through working in a hospital, and wanting to become a doctor. It was always on my mind. Several years later, I recall spending $7 on a pack while travelling in New York, and still…I smoked.

How much money had I spent over the years on something that I knew was shortening my life? Comedians of the times would brag about their smoking conquests, stating it was the LAST ten years of their lives they would miss out on, the diaper-wearing stage…I thought I was so cool, but also thought about how weak I was being addicted to something so small and light-weight; something that years later as an adult would have me standing outside in a snowstorm, freezing, just to have a quick puff, because smoking inside was taboo.

In my twenties, I dated two women who would not tolerate smoking. Thank God for the nicotine patch. I was able to hide my addiction from each of them...for a short period of time. I really did want to quit. I almost did one time – lasting six weeks at one point. An argument and subsequent break-up led me right back to that *old friend,* the cigarette. *He* was always there for me. Do you ever feel that way about cigarettes, booze, or something deep down inside you know you should quit? I did. Jumping in a cab, I took a ride to the closest gas station, just to *take the edge off.* There *he* was after this silly little argument with a girlfriend. *I would just have one cigarette,* I told myself. Then, just like that, I was back full-time. I was smoking about a pack and a half to two packs a day in no time. This continued for years.

At my sister's house in Florida, in my mid-30's, I realized I had spent more than half my life with a dangling, burning, disgusting, stinking cigarette in my mouth. There is a HUGE difference between West Coast (where I used to live and smoked a couple of packs of cigarettes a day) and Midwest or even East Coast smokers. On the West Coast, most smokers step outside, opting not to smoke in the house. The weather — the heat/humidity in Florida and cold/snow in the Midwest (the two other places I'd lived) — dictated and almost demanded smoking inside. In Florida, my sister and her husband smoked indoors. Due to Florida's nearly year-round blistering heat and humidity, they had their house hermetically sealed, trying to keep the air conditioning inside and the weather out.

> I spent half my life with a disgusting, stinking cigarette dangling from my mouth.

Upon my arrival, I began to smoke inside, too. It did not take long to notice my niece, at 11 years of age, had one of the most pronounced smoker's coughs I had ever heard. That golden giggle that could make the hardest of hearts melt was gone, replaced with hacking and gasping. It was as if she had been an unwanted recipient of a lung transplant from a coal miner. I did not want to contribute to this. However, quitting was still one of the furthest things from my mind.

One thing was for sure, I would go outside as much as possible to keep my cigarette smoke away from my niece. My stay here was not just about cigarettes, but also re-launching my life. When it came to employment, being in Florida was not much different than being in Indiana. I still didn't have the skill set people were looking for, and I was incredibly independent, not fitting well into the typical office environment. Phone calls were made and resumes were sent, but I still wasn't getting any offers. The living situation was different and should have caused me to set a better example, but the spiraling pity party I was having didn't allow me to do that. I no longer had a bed to sleep on like at my brother's place, but a blow-up mattress instead. I no longer had the privacy I was afforded in my brother's basement, so had to be physically present more. With these changes, especially being around my 11-year-old niece, I *should have* been better, but I wasn't. At the very least, I did decide to take control back in one area of my life: my addiction to cigarettes. I made a decision that would positively impact me for the rest of my life: *I would quit smoking*. But, how? When I had failed so many times in the past?

Smoking was something I had picked up a couple of times before it took hold, but once it did, cigarettes figuratively took a "death grip" on my life and wouldn't let go for years. After sneaking cigarettes now and then from my mother's packs around the apartment, smoking really took hold for me when I was 15. It is weird to think about now, but many people pick up the habit in their early and mid-teens, when it's not even legal to purchase them. And although not legal to buy cigarettes as a young teenager, smoking becomes such a strong habit. I found there were always ways to get my hands on cigarettes. Years later, I would notice people without any means and living on the streets were able to find ways to get their hands on smokes.

At 35 years of age, I had to face facts: I WAS addicted and I had been smoking/killing myself for more than 20 years. For over half my life, I had been harming myself and others by sucking on tar, carcinogens, fire, and extreme heat. The combination of spending time with my niece and hearing her smoker's cough at the age of 11, knowing I couldn't run half a mile without my side feeling like it was on fire as I gasped for breath, and overall disappointment with lack of control over my own thoughts and actions, let me know it was well beyond time to make a change.

I knew it was time for a change, but my internal voice (like yours may be, too) was amazingly difficult to ignore. If you are like me, sometimes I am amazed at how negative my brain can be. *I can't because…(insert lame excuse here).* My loudest, hard to tune out internal thoughts would start up each time I encountered someone who *had* quit smoking. These people who had successfully quit smoking wouldn't even need to be on a soapbox about quitting before my brain had played out the entire sequence. This just might sound familiar to some of you. As soon as someone would begin telling me how they quit, my negative self-talk began. Had I actually been able to listen to them and hear their story, it may have really helped me. But, my internal (or even external, as I may have cut them off) voice was already saying:

> *"Yeah, I'm glad YOU quit, BUT I could NEVER quit. You only smoked X amount of cigarettes, where I smoke 1.5 to 2 packs per day, so it's different,"* or, *"You only smoke when you have a cocktail or in the*

evening. I smoke all day, actually, I've already lit one before I'm out of bed in the morning, so it's different...I could NEVER quit," or whatever the excuse was at the time.

Does any of this sound familiar to you? The truth of the matter is it's NOT different – you either smoke or you don't. So, like me, you or the loved one you are encouraging to quit just needs to realize there are hundreds of thousands...no...millions of people who HAVE quit whether they smoke 1 or 100 cigarettes a day! What this means is you (or they) can too! You are just as strong-willed and capable as those who have quit smoking before you.

So, how did I actually quit? Simple...I got a "degree" in quitting. Not just a degree, but a doctorate in quitting. That's right, I am now David Ross, "PhD," when it comes to quitting. I bet you didn't even know you could get a degree in quitting, did you? Now hold on...before I lose anyone to their internal voice or thoughts to a *degree? A doctorate? I don't have time for that! I cannot afford to go back to school,* OR whatever might be sounding off in your head right now, let me explain. I'm talking about our internal voices. Your internal voice can be reprogrammed or rewired...seriously, who is in control of that? YOU are. Let me help you with what that means.

First, what do I mean about getting a "PhD" in quitting? I heard someone talking about "**Pig-Headed Determination**" one day, and how he used this philosophy to grow his business. It clicked for me...that was the PhD I needed. I just had to be stronger than the inanimate object I wanted to quit (in this case a feeble cigarette) AND have a *new* message playing in my head each time I wanted to smoke.

> **Pig-Headed Determination**

I had to be determined like never before. I re-programed myself to think thoughts like, *I'm every bit as strong and capable as these other people,* or *if they can quit, so can I.* Or, to really simplify things, I started thinking about the difference in size between me (at the time a 225 pound human being with a brain) vs. a tiny little cigarette with no brain. It cannot think, reason, plot, scheme, or plan. It just sits there. I began to realize this is the silliest thing…a cigarette trying to get *me* to bend to its will? Oh wait, it doesn't have a *will,* because it's just a thing.

Do you see how a simple shift in thinking can empower you? This may sound too easy or maybe just plain stupid, "airy," new-age, or whatever to some. I assure you though, if your internal voice is SCREAMING at you right now about how you CAN'T do what I did, ask yourself why that is. Why do you *think* you cannot do what I did? What you tell yourself is important, so don't defeat yourself before you begin, especially since I haven't even laid out the plan yet.

Give it a chance. This just may work for you, and if it's not the "right" way for you, there IS a "right" way which you just might find by joining the movement at www.ifinallyquit.com and connecting with another successful quitter. There is more than one way to defeat a cigarette.

7

That's It, I Quit. I'm Movin' On

How I finally quit smoking and the birth of IFQ, Inc.

I had heard of people *visualizing* and *seeing* themselves doing things, but my analytical mind could not quite wrap itself around that concept. I tried to *see* myself doing things, but did not have the clear vision I thought I needed. I was under the impression I should be able to close my eyes, concentrate and *see* things as well as if I had my eyes open. I was disappointed and mainly discouraged that I could not *see* the way I thought I should be able to. So, I developed visual aids to help me to *see* at all times.

I thought I could get these visual aids or images into my subconscious by thinking about them or viewing them many times throughout the day. And, guess what…I could. I found I could produce *visions* of quitting by inundating my surroundings with helpful reminders of quitting. It became clear I COULD *see* these images when I closed my eyes or at night in my dreams.

The Visual System that worked (and still works) for me…

I used the internet to find images and pictures that portrayed quitting. I downloaded tons of "quitting" pictures and used them as scrolling pictures for my screensaver on my laptop. I printed them and posted them on the wall around the room. It was at this time I received *the vision* for "I Finally Quit" (IFQ). I began to work on the prototype of the logo that is now a huge part of my life, and hopefully, soon to be yours (if not already).

The countdown…

I picked a quit date. For me, my quit date was just five days away. I used common sense to remind myself that people quit doing things all the time. Although I already knew many people struggle with quitting, and so had I in the past, I believed I would not need to struggle this time. Once my quit date was solidified in my mind, I began to really focus.

For five days, the first things I would see upon waking were the "quitting" images scrolling on my laptop, and they were the last images I would see before drifting off to sleep. Throughout the day I would pull up the images to see at random times. Although I had begun to slightly modify my behavior by smoking a little less or at different times, I was still smoking at least a pack and a half a day. I allowed this to be *okay*. It didn't matter that I hadn't significantly cut back or slowed down yet, because I had accepted a quit date (this "acceptance" would become very important when I later decided to quit drinking). Taking those days preparing myself to quit helped to reduce the pressure on myself.

With just four days to go…

I continued to use the inspirational images on my computer. I would take breaks from working and pull the images up on my monitor. I would think about what it would be like to *not* be chained to cigarettes for a day, for a month, for the rest of my life. This is when I really discovered that my brain could not "see" or not visualize me *not* smoking! Go back and reread that…it's profound. This was a huge, triumphant breakthrough for my mindset.

We cannot "*not think*" of something. To think of myself *not* smoking, I first HAD to think of me smoking. It is like trying to *not* think of orange juice being in the refrigerator. Seriously, think about that. What do you see? Orange juice, right? For there not to be orange juice in there, you have to think about (and imagine) orange juice being there first! So, instead of me trying to visualize myself *not* smoking, I visualized myself stamping out a cigarette or throwing one on the ground. I began to think of times when I was smoking and would walk away from cigarettes for good.

I put this thought process to work…I thought about past times when I would travel, flying to a new city for work. I would get to my hotel, open up my suitcase, and smell "clean" clothes that reeked of stale cigarette smoke. I thought of having to stand outside in sub-zero, freezing temperatures just to have a quick drag. I thought of all sorts of times where I was embarrassed, disappointed, or uncomfortable because of smoking. I could feel a shift in my thinking. It was time for bed. I focused on the developing IFQ logo, the images on my monitor, and those posted on the wall as I turned out the light.

With just three days to go…

I awoke to the same images I drifted off to. Something was definitely going to be different this time. I could feel myself taking personal responsibility for my actions and for my desire to quit. I *knew* I was going to change my thinking and my actions. This new-found personal responsibility was definitely going to help, but I felt like I needed just a little more "oomph" to hold my feet to the fire. So, I enlisted the help of my 11-year-old niece. I decided to draft a contract that not only would hold me personally and financially responsible to quitting, but also have her commit to never having to be in my situation.

I realized I was spending about $5.00 per pack on cigarettes and smoking about a pack and a half a day — that's $7.50 a day — and I was struggling at a new job. There were many days that I was not even making that much in a day, but somehow I found a way to feed the habit anyway. I wrote up a simple contract: for every day that my niece and I did not smoke, I would contribute $1.50 to a quitting fund and eventually give it to her.

Here I was, making a promise to myself and my niece to continually spend money on this habit in order to remind myself of where I once was. These contributions to the no-smoking fund would accumulate for her starting from age 11 until she turned 18. A $1.50 a day may not sound like much money, although it's definitely less than I would spend had I continued to smoke. But like I mentioned, I was homeless and had no funds to be buying these stupid things anyway.

Uncle David & Ivy's No Smoking Agreement

Uncle David agrees to give Ivy $1.50 every day from her 11.5 birthday to her 18th birthday, if Ivy agrees to not smoke cigarettes or take any other drugs. The agreed upon dollar amount of $3,360 will be paid upon Ivy's 18th birthday.

_____   _____
Uncle David   Ivy Ross

Dated: 2007

I did some quick math and realized $3,360 was a lot of money to me…and even more to a teenager. The thought of how much I would spend if I did not stop was even more staggering. Now I had a purpose greater than myself for quitting, and found someone to hold me accountable; someone I cared about. Is there someone in your life you can have hold you accountable? Do you have kids? Siblings? Friends? Take it from me, someone who has felt completely alone in life at times, there *is* someone. A higher power? An organization you can enter into a similar contract with, like I did with my niece? Ultimately, I knew I would be helping not just myself, but her as well.

One other thing I began to do at this point was begin to modify my behavior. It wasn't anything drastic, yet – that would come soon enough. The slight change I started to incorporate with three days to go was simple: each time I went to light up, I would stare at and really concentrate on my IFQ logo prototype. I would think about the great feeling I would have when I was finally free from cigarettes. Even though I was still smoking, with each cigarette, I was thinking about quitting. This seems like a simple little change…and it is. As you focus on quitting, take this book with you. Look at the quitting images and logos at www.ifinallyquit.com. Join the community, connect with others, and quit…something.

With just two days to go…

I decided it was time to really make a financial commitment. Not just a hypothetical or a contract with a youngster, but I really decided to hit myself where it hurt…my wallet. Remember, I barely had any money at the time, but was still finding a way to buy cigarettes a couple of packs at a time. I went to the store and purchased all eight weeks of the nicotine patches used by millions of people to quit smoking. This is substantial: the patches cost more than buying 40 packs of cigarettes! Regardless of your financial state, committing more than a hundred dollars to quitting is substantial. This was really starting to take shape in my mind.

I was beginning to *own* it. I now had accepted a change in my thinking *and* my behavior. I had committed to not smoking for eight weeks. For more than half my life—20 years—I had never gone eight weeks without a cigarette. Half of my life had been about breathing polluted, stinky air that had prevented me from being in certain social situations, dating this girl or that, and hiding my behavior from employers and those I respected.

It was this acceptance that led me to the *switch* in my mind. I realized I would need to "flip this switch" mentally in just a couple of days. In order for me to turn off the smoking switch, I had to accept that the switch existed. I knew such a switch *did* exist, as I had witnessed my ex-fiancé flip a similar switch in her mind just over a year ago, when she changed her life by incorporating biking and running into her fitness routine.

So many things in life are really just in our heads. If we'd just let go of believing that what exists now is etched in stone forever, we can truly unlock our greatness. And, that is what I did. I accepted the fact that such a switch was there... somewhere. With each passing moment, with each new cigarette, with each new stinking butt, I was a step closer to achieving my goal. I wanted to be a quitter, and this time, I accepted that I was a quitter.

With just one day to go...

If you plan on doing exactly what I did to quit, I ask you to exhibit extreme caution with this step I'm about to explain. Not just with cigarettes, but anything you plan on quitting. Keep in mind, this step can (and should) be completely metaphorical! I went for the literal interpretation though, and for smoking cigarettes, this can be highly effective. But, for drinking, harder drugs, and many other behaviors, this could have you ending up in jail or worse, dead. Again, use extreme caution.

I awoke to my new routine of looking at all the images throughout my room and on my monitor. I had been downloading and printing more each day over the last week. The images were posted everywhere in my room. If I had my own apartment or home, these pictures would have been posted on every wall and every surface. As you already know, I was smoking at least a pack and a half a day, but it was not uncommon for me to polish off two packs. On this final day of smoking, I would take that quantity to a whole new level. I decided to smoke five packs on my last day as a smoker.

With the sunrise, as I lit my *last* first cigarette of the day, I planned out my last smoking day. I got out three, full packs of my "light" brand, the "full-flavored" and menthol packs I had bought the day before, and the five clove cigarettes I took from my sister's packs (I wonder if she ever missed them). I carried these five packs and five cloves around with me everywhere I went throughout the house. I remember how awkward it was fumbling around with them throughout the day. I was constantly smoking that last day. It is difficult to smoke over 100 cigarettes in a day. My stomach churned and my face turned green several times as I constantly lit cigarette after cigarette. I was not just lighting them to light them, I was smoking them, sucking in all of the toxicity I possibly could.

The full-flavored and menthol cigarettes burned my chest and throat immediately. I would work those in between my normal load of light cigarettes, constantly inhaling the toxic fumes. The flavors and the burning were disgusting, but nothing had prepared me for that first clove cigarette. This was absolutely the most pungent and disgusting thing I had ever smoked. Throughout this last day, there would be many times I wanted to put an end to the ridiculousness of the amount I was smoking, but I had a plan and nothing was going to stop me from completing it. I tend to obsess over the smallest of details, so although I desired greatly to be a "quitter" that day, I felt compelled to stick to my bizarre plan.

I smoked all day long. I remember sitting alone, after everyone had come home from school or work, watched television, had dinner, and had gone to bed. There I sat...alone and smoking into the wee hours of the morning. As I snubbed out my last butt, completing all 105 cigarettes for the day, I was absolutely nauseated. Satisfied I had completed my pre-quitting plan, I went to bed feeling sick and smelling like a chimney, hopefully for the very last time.

On my quit day...

I woke to the same images, reminding me today however, that I *had* quit. No more quitting to come, but *this* was the day I would quit. I placed my first patch on my deltoid muscle of my left shoulder and went about my day. Something was definitely different. Each time my body wanted to reach for a cigarette and go through the routine of smoking, instead I looked at my IFQ logo and those of other images I had downloaded. I would remind myself of the "switch" I had found in my brain. *I can do this.* All I had to do was not go through the routine of lighting up. I was forced to think about when and why I wanted to light up: answering the phone, going outside, having a drink, after a meal, etc...and I realized it was just a habit of "when" and "why" to smoke. I did not miss smoking, but the *action* that it was coupled with!

> **I didn't miss smoking, but I missed the action smoking was coupled with.**

In the late afternoon of the first day that I FINALLY QUIT smoking, I knew I had done it. On that very first day, I *knew* it!

I removed the patch and felt a relief I had never known. I exhaled and felt what *FINALLY* felt like. It was kind of like one of those days when you stare into the perfectly blue sky and watch wispy clouds drift, and you can sense eternity...you just know it's there. This relief led to a calm and an acceptance I had been missing for 20 years.

The next day, I returned the six weeks of the patches I had not opened (they wouldn't take back the one box with one patch missing). Believe me when I tell you, due to my financial situation, I was completely relieved they took *any* of them back for a refund. It would take me another four years to implement the same system to quit drinking, but would I have the strength, courage, and will power to do it? As you may know by now, it nearly cost me my life...but one more thing of note here. Many people who struggle to quit smoking tend to say they can't do it while they continue to drink alcohol or while still drinking coffee. That's absolutely not true. Although those two behaviors feel completely intertwined, they are two separate acts: 1. smoking, and 2. drinking.

Think about when you began smoking (if you did). For most of us, we were way too young to be drinking alcohol. So, they were not one combined act and still aren't. A person just has to make up their own mind they are going to quit. You CAN quit anything, just as you began them, just like I did and millions have. So, get to it...make a plan, then stick to it.

In the days that followed...

I made it through my second day as a non-smoker with no cessation aid...no patch, no pill, no fake vapor cigarette: just me and my desire not to fail. I didn't want to be seen as a *loser* in my niece's eyes. I would just have to stick to the plan. With each craving, I would tell myself it would pass. At this time, I didn't have a support system other than the paper contract I'd made with my niece. I was still ashamed of my *homeless* situation and sleeping on the floor in the spare room at my sister's place. In this state, there was no one for me to reach out to...due to my shame. I avoided all social media, because I didn't want to tell people I had no money, no *real* job, and no prospects. I longed to be able to talk to someone...anyone about the cravings...but, here was the interesting thing: the cravings past – each and every time. Every 15 or 20 minutes, I'd think about cigarettes for a minute or two and then forget about them. This would go on for days and each time, the increment between cravings grew a little bit longer.

I suppose I could have blogged about my experience, but back then, I didn't know what a blog was. I didn't know of any social media groups dedicated to helping others. But, I sure wished one existed. And then, BAM, it hit me...why not create a website that would empower other people to feel this exact same RELIEF that I now had of knowing "I Finally Quit"?

I began reworking the IFQ logo and documenting what I thought the website should do. I had no expertise and certainly no money to make it happen, but I had a desire. The desire grew stronger every day that I was in Florida living at my sister's place. She and my brother-in-law continued to smoke in the house, and why not? It was their house. They shouldn't have to stop or change their actions or behaviors just because I decided I'd had enough of smoking. I would simply go outside and take a walk from time to time, when the smoke in the house became too much to bear.

For any of you who have ever quit (and ultimately not

succeeded) or are in the process of quitting smoking for the first time as you read this, you know being around that stinky, irritating, disgusting cigarette smoke is somehow oddly appealing. With everything we know is wrong with smoking, when you are early in the quitting process, it's somehow inviting. Let me take a moment to encourage you, and remind you that you CAN do this. Think of what led you to that "quitting" moment. Why do you want it? Focus on that for a few seconds and the cravings will pass.

I had a new-found focus. This was it. I now had to focus on not only building ifinallyquit.com and building a platform that would help and inspire others, but I also had to increase my income. I began to work with an online company based out of California selling business to business software. Most of the reps went "door to door and floor to floor." I visited as many businesses in a day as possible. I was without a car and 3000 miles from the company's headquarters. I had to come up with an entirely new marketing plan that would work specifically for me. Somehow, during my first month with the company, I qualified for the monthly bonus they offered. I had never been very good at selling over the phone. I had tried in the past, but this time, because of the urgency to get back to having my own place and wanting to create this website, I dialed and dialed, then dialed some more.

After several years of struggling, I finally had a little bit of money coming my way, allowing me to at least get off the floor of my sister's spare bedroom. I reached out to some friends in Southern California and found a place I could stay as I continued to rebuild. I wish this was the point in this story where I could say all of my struggles were 100% behind me, and that life was great again. I wish I could say that I started making better decisions, but that just wasn't the case. I did have to get out of Florida though.

Even with being somewhat of a "role model" or inspiration for my niece because of quitting smoking, the fact remained I was drinking bourbon at an alarming rate. Had I stayed, I wouldn't be remembered for quitting smoking, but for something much darker...I was sure of that.

8

Sanitarium

September 2007 (San Diego)

Arriving back in San Diego felt great at first. I felt like I was getting closer to regaining my independence. However, independence would still be years away. Although I had made the bonus commission during the first month with this new company, closing ten accounts a month (every month) turned out to be extremely difficult. I was not making enough money to cover my rent. I decided enough was enough, and I would MAKE something happen. Sitting on the floor in my rented room "dialing for dollars" just wasn't going to cut it. *This isn't who I am*, I'd tell myself. The shame, embarrassment and even more self-doubt than I'd had up until now were welling up inside. I would focus on my negative moments and low points over the last few years, and completely ignore the fact that I was still…here. I was still alive and breathing. I had continually refused to give up. At this time though, positive thoughts were the furthest from my mind, and I was approaching my darkest hours.

I focused on everything that was wrong with my life. I hadn't fully faced the reality of my "disengagement" with such a beautiful woman. It had now been years of wandering from couch to basement to floors to random overnight stays in public parks my family didn't even know about. (I'd go off on an overnight drinking "bender" and sleep wherever I happened to pass out.) I still had nowhere near the income I was used to, and I was still drunk. When all of these thoughts came together, it was almost too much to bare. I became severely depressed. I was in some very dark places of my mind. As I faced most of this alone, I wasn't sure I'd rebound to live a happy and successful life. My shame and embarrassment of failure still prevented me from really inviting everyone from my past or anyone new into my life.

Although I'd taken a few steps *forward* with new-found income, a new place to lay my head, and putting cigarettes behind me, I still knew life wasn't *right*. I'd sit on the floor in my room with no furniture, and ask myself, *"Were things really getting better?"* After two years of bouncing around the country and feeling worthless, I was not focusing on the positive steps I'd taken forward to be back in San Diego, but only on those I had taken backward.

Being in such a negative, dark place in my mind had turned me suicidal. It didn't seem like that long ago I was one of the most positive, upbeat people, ever. After a couple of weeks in this new home, I had devised a couple of ways to end my life, and I was nearly ready to take action. I won't go into specifics here, but I had two, fairly elaborate plans. I went so far as to call my brother and father to say goodbye. On a whim and with no real reasoning behind it (other than Divine intervention), I placed a call to an ex-colleague, before I was to end it all.

> **My thoughts turned suicidal. I devised two potential plans to end my life.**

When we spoke, I told her of my desperation. She let me know about a three-day, transformational, self-improvement seminar workshop she'd been to recently, and how it had changed the course of her life. She was convinced it would save me too, turning my *lack* into a life of success and abundance. There were two things I knew for sure at this point...she was way too happy on whatever Kool-Aid she was drinking, and I wanted nothing to do with it, especially once I heard the cost to attend was nearly $500! Hearing my frustration and being so convinced this was what I needed, she put up the money herself to get me to go. Just a few days later, I found myself in a hotel conference room with 150 other people who wanted something more from life. Can I just tell you, not all of these people were down and out – most of them were not. In fact, most of them seemed rather happy. But, I found myself not wanting to be around the overall joy and excitement in that room...at least initially.

During the next three days, my thinking shifted, and I did get back on track. I wish I could tell you they waived a magic wand and all the attendees were transformed into new beings, or that I quit drinking over that three-day course. However, that wasn't the case. There would be a lot of work to do, and mainly it centered on changing "the stories and programs" that were running in each of our minds. I was energized and reminded that I am an awesome creation of God, made in His image. I had the power of His universe in my hands and mind. I could create anything I wanted and needed. How did I know this was possible? Well, I'd seen God work many times in my life. With His help I'd done some amazing things and created money out of thin air before, so why couldn't I do it now?

This was it...just like I KNEW in that moment that I had finally quit smoking...I KNEW the days of lack and struggle were over.

9

Oops!...I Did it Again

Just a couple of days after attending the workshop, instead of making sales calls, I decided to spend an hour or more talking on the phone with an acquaintance in Los Angeles about the struggles and difficulties I had been having in life. He was telling me of his struggles and how he wanted something different, too. This conversation turned out to be a "BAM" moment, putting me on a path that would be a real game changer for me. This story will have you saying "No way!" out loud again, but first, let's recap.

Remember, just a few years prior, I'd had it *all* (or so I thought): a condo, a fiancé, money, freedom, and an extremely unhealthy lifestyle. I'd lost all of that, except for the unhealthy lifestyle, guzzling nearly a fifth of bourbon every day at this point. And remember, that's the equivalent of 17 beers or four bottles of wine...a day! I'd couch-surfed around Southern California, hid in my brother's basement, slept on the floor of my sister's spare bedroom, and made it back to San Diego, just to contemplate and almost execute suicide. Now, I was feeling energized, believing that things were just about to turn the corner. By the way, this *fateful* phone call turned out to be the person who would become my assistant and accompany me to the ICU in San Francisco.

During that call, I was very specific about being sick and tired of this struggle. "Life was never this way before and it isn't designed to be," I recall saying. I reminisced about my previous job and life as a seminar leader, which allowed me to visit all 50 states and really experience the country while making fairly decent money. Then I said I wanted even more this time. I wanted and would find a job that allowed me to travel the world, not just the country. This job would not only come with a driver to get me from point A to point B, but a pilot to fly me around and a captain to traverse the seas, making it possible for me to continue to drink as much as my body and mind could handle. This job would provide twice the amount of the highest annual income I had ever earned before. By the time I was done affirming everything I wanted and everything I was, I felt a great weight lifting off of me. There was not just a glimmer of hope, but I felt as if a spotlight was shining on me, and I *did* matter. Now this next part you are going to think I am making up, but I swear to you it is the truth.

That very evening, my friend's mother came home (I was renting a room from a friend's mother) and she sat down on the couch next to me. She said, "I know you are having a hard time paying me rent, and I know you are looking for another job. Today I was doing a little extra cleaning and found this employment section of the newspaper under a couch. Maybe there is something in here for you." I opened it as she was still talking. On about the third page, an ad was almost pulsating right off the page. The ad read, "Not Your Average 9-to-5 Job: Travel the world and earn well over $100,000 a year!" It had my attention. *Go on...*, I could hear my internal voice say.

The ad continued to list requirements and skills they were looking for, and I'm not kidding, the only thing missing from the requirements was my name, date of birth, and social security number. It was exactly what I had just said I wanted a couple of hours earlier. The very next day I called the number, and they bypassed nearly the entire interview process and pretty much offered me the position right then, *sight unseen*. Had they seen (what I had no idea others could see at the time) how alcohol was tearing my body apart, they probably would have never made the offer.

> No way! This was exactly what I said I wanted a couple hours ago.

Here's the position. Nearly 80% of the cruise ships have an art gallery on them and most of them employ an auctioneer. Although at the time I knew nothing of art, one month later, I was wrapping up training in the Detroit, Michigan area as the company's top prospect. Of all the new trainees who made it through their program, they offered me first choice of any ship I wanted. I wasn't too surprised. For some reason, my ego had completely forgotten the last two years of lack, struggle, and self-doubt. Some of my arrogance from years past was returning, and that was about to cause serious problems with my progress. I chose a cruise line that was known for attracting people of means, as opposed to a line known for 20-something's who wanted to consume their weight in beer during a three to five day cruise.

Remember how specific I was when I was "conjuring" up this job? What did I want? A pilot, a driver, a captain, money, freedom, and more…right? Within 24 hours of leaving Detroit, I'd end up in my own hotel room in Tortola, a British-Virgin Island, then onto the cruise liner. The journey included travel by planes, taxis, and joining my first ship. I had an expense account for food and booze and the freedom to roam the ship and ports, which many employees of the cruise industry never receive.

The position would have me living on a cruise ship and selling product from port to port, plus my own drivers and captains so

I could see the world...AMAZING! Even my own room stocked full of wine and booze on the cruise liner! What could possibly go wrong?! After record sales for that particular ship — selling more in four days than the previous person in my position had produced in a month — I was kicked off of the ship after just ten days. How did that happen? I mentioned my loneliness...right? Combine that with some arrogance and pride, and I was on a path to disaster.

I had a lot of energy that had been building inside of me that escaped in a matter of days, while working this new job. This positon required me to be the *life of the party*. Easy! I offered free champagne and spa services to potential big spenders along with invitations to wine parties. I got to be the *host* of the parties...something I dearly missed from my condo days in downtown San Diego, when I could splurge and pick up the bar tab for my friends. On the ship and in port, I was encouraged to go mingle and build relationships with potential clients while exploring the ports and foreign countries.

Late one afternoon, five or six days into my new job, I found myself sitting alone in a bar in St. Croix. Nothing new about sitting alone in a bar for me...except I was in St. Croix ...hello! The American dollar still went a long way there, and good thing – I hadn't gotten my first paycheck yet. There were signs up all around the bar advertising their bourbon special that wouldn't begin till *happy hour*. After very little negotiating with the bartender, he was pouring bourbon on the rocks at the reduced pricing, just for me. So, I sat and drank discounted bourbon for hours.

Knowing I had to get back to the ship, I settled my tab and began to make my way back. On the walk, I noticed two beautiful women walking just ahead of me, so I quickened my steps to catch up. "How are you ladies enjoying your vacation?" I asked. They responded they were having the time of their lives. "Me too," I said. We continued our conversation on the way back to the ship. They took interest in me when I let them know I worked on the ship, and even more interest when I told them I could get them wine and spa treatments if they were interested.

> I craved conversation from the opposite sex.

We boarded the ship together and headed straight for one of the many bars onboard, where I could comp them some drinks. Getting to know the "Boston Babes" (not my name for them, but nearly every single man and some married men had come up with the moniker for them) was fantastic. I craved conversation from the opposite sex. I'd been cooped up in basements, sleeping on floors and couches of other people's homes, following their rules for years. But now, I was free to do what I wanted, when I wanted...or so I thought. There was one rule and one rule only for a person who held my position on the cruise liner; one simple rule, really. I was not supposed to cross the threshold of a guest room. It makes sense for guest safety and to protect employees from wrongful accusations. What I did not know at the time was that the inside of guest rooms were just about the only areas on a ship without cameras rolling 24/7. Seriously, these cruise ships have as many hidden cameras as a casino in Las Vegas or the vaults of Fort Knox!

We made plans to go our separate ways for a couple of hours, before meeting back up for dinner. Chivalry is important to me, so of course, I walked them back to their room, helping them with the bags of clothing and souvenirs they'd bought while on the island. When we got to their suite, I made sure to stay outside of the room. They insisted I come in and join them for another cocktail before going back to my room. I thanked them, but explained the one rule the ship had, and I was still new to my position, and didn't want to *rock the boat*. Ha ha...pun intended. Well, *rock the boat* is truly what they had in mind as they both enticed me to come inside. I really wish I could tell you the gentlemanly nature in me allowed me to walk away, but after years of isolation, I entered their room.

The next few days, I was completely out of control – intoxicated and reckless. The "Boston Babes" and I spent every moment together when I wasn't working. Even when I was working, they would stop by the one of many champagne parties I was hosting. The attention I was receiving from them did not go unnoticed, and it didn't take long for jealousy to spread rampantly throughout the ship. Here I was finally in a position to get out of the financial and emotional hole I'd dug for years, and I was about to blow the whole thing up.

A couple of days later, the ship's captain informed me I'd be asked to leave the ship when we arrived back in the States and had already notified my employers. They had me dead to rights with video of me and the "Boston Babes" all over that ship. I made it a point to enjoy the last few days on the ship as if I were a guest and not an employee. A frightfully bad series of decisions made during my last, booze-infused days on the ship.

Saturday morning—at precisely 6:20am—security was knocking on the door of my room. They escorted me off the ship, whisking me away in the darkness of the early morning before any of the guests were allowed to disembark. There I was in Miami, Florida, with no money, bad credit, no job, and nowhere to go. You may be shaking your head and saying, "No way!" That last line may even sound familiar to some of you as the opening credit lines from the television series *Burn Notice*…but, yes, that was me, *burned* with absolutely nowhere to go.

I'd exhausted my welcome at my sister's in Tampa. I'd caused undue stress on my brother's marriage and family back in

Indiana. I was, beyond a shadow of a doubt, a drunk and a loser making incredibly bad decisions. *Where would I go?* And, would I begin down the path to getting sober so I could make better decisions? At this point, not a chance. You've probably heard that some people need to hit rock bottom before they can recover or rebound, right? Well, I just didn't think there was any further left to sink, but that fateful day with the ER and ICU was still a little over three years away.

I called the employer's headquarters in Detroit and convinced them to front me some of the money from the commissions I was owed from the past ten days of working for them. They agreed to buy me a plane ticket to Tampa (where my sister lived) so I could get my bearings, then another ticket to wherever I wanted within the next couple of days. They'd simply deduct the cost from the commission they were set to pay me in the next couple of weeks. Also, they would wait a couple of days to let me know my services would no longer be necessary and there would not be another ship for me to join. With a sense of false security, and knowing I wouldn't have to sleep on the streets of Miami, I made my way to the airport, where I proceeded to drink with reckless abandon.

My sister was good enough to let me stay for two days while I scrambled to figure out my next move. My brother let me know he could pick me up at the airport in Indiana, but he and his wife had made the uncomfortable decision to not allow me to stay at their home. So, I booked the flight to Indiana knowing I was running out of time and chances to get my life turned around.

10

Way Down in Old Indiana

January 2008 (Berne, IN)

After picking me up from the airport in Fort Wayne, Indiana, my brother drove me to Berne, Indiana (population 3,800). Berne is the tight-knit community where I'd gone to high school and couldn't wait to get away from nearly two decades prior. And, Berne is where I was best man for my friend's wedding. Well, there I stood, at his doorstep, hoping he'd take me in. I was greeted with open arms and no judgment – just a warm place for me to settle in for the winter. Within a couple of days, I had a phone line brought in and an internet connection established and got back to work with the company I'd started with a few months back. Even more determined than before, I *had* to make it back to California and out of Indiana.

Because gossip travels so fast through a small community like this, I did everything I could to minimize my presence there even though I knew there would be many people who would take me in and give me shelter had I asked. But, my embarrassment and shame kept me from letting many know I was even there. I can tell you the few people who knew I was there showed me love and generosity beyond anything I can express here. Not everyone was working, employment was still difficult to come by, but I never went without a meal, a shower, or a warm place to lay my head. I also didn't go without a drink. Most of the time I could afford to buy a bottle of something, but if not, my friends were always quick to make sure my drinking addiction was *taken care of*.

Speaking of having something to drink, at a bar one evening, I bumped into an old friend who would get me back in touch with someone I hadn't seen in more than 15 years. What happened next shows the true compassion of the human heart.

Fifteen years prior, just after college, a friend of mine whom I'd graduated high school with told me of an opportunity to move in with and share a home with three young ladies who were finishing up their degrees. *Three female roommates?!* Of course I jumped at the chance.

All these years later, this woman heard I was back in Indiana and struggling financially. Within 24 hours, she and her husband (whom I'd never met) were on the road, making the two hour drive from Indianapolis to Berne to seek me out. We caught up with each other's lives and experiences from the last 15 years. It was great to hear myself tell of successes, especially with all of the disasters I'd created and poor judgment I'd shown in many circumstances the past few years.

The shining highlight of my story was the fact I'd quit smoking and had an overwhelming desire to quit drinking and other detrimental behaviors. And, more importantly, I wanted to create a platform that would inspire others to quit behaviors that held them back. Later that evening, after the two of them had talked with each other and prayed about my situation, they opened their home to me. Being in a much bigger city like Indianapolis provided many more opportunities for me to grow my business to business software sales portfolio. I thanked those in Berne who had protected and sheltered me, then made my way to the *big city*.

Upon moving in with this couple, they knew of my desire to help others find inspiration to quit, too. However, I hadn't filled them in on one part of the human psyche that I wanted to help others overcome. This more than likely would have been a deal breaker had they known. My plan over the next four years (not that I anticipated living with them for that long) was to continue consuming a minimum of a fifth of bourbon every day until my 40th birthday. Why would I set such an insanely detrimental "goal" for myself? It really stemmed from my idea of quitting and the negative thinking that ran in my mind regarding quitting.

I already explained my past reasons why I couldn't quit smoking, because *I smoked more than the person who had been able to quit*, or *how my situation was different than theirs*, etc. These are real internal thought processes that many people deal with. I wanted to take that argument or reasoning away from people who I hoped to help one day. I wanted to connect with people in a way that would not cause their internal voice or thoughts to be...*It won't work* or *I can't*. I really wanted people to know that I drank excessively, so they wouldn't think I didn't *understand*. I certainly didn't want someone to think they drank more than me.

> **My insanely detrimental goal:
> Drink a fifth of bourbon every day so no one can ever say I don't understand.**

I didn't want the same type of negative thinking I'd employed over the years to prevent someone from successfully quitting. I wanted the shock value of being able to say I drank a fifth of bourbon every day for five years then quit...just like that. I felt as though I could find a similar "switch" in my mind for alcohol, and just turn it off on my 40th birthday. As you know, my body did not make it that long, but my commitment and compulsion to that level of consumption was now underway.

It couldn't have been easy to have someone staying under their roof who was drinking bourbon non-stop, and I am sure I gave them numerous reasons to be concerned. During this time, I learned (and really tried) to be silent as I moved throughout their house while they were home. I made a game of quietly moving around in the evenings and late at night, learning which floorboards creak and which would allow for silent passage back to the refrigerator for more ice and alcohol. For the most part, I made sure not to begin consuming drinks until the noon hour. However, with them being away at work, they wouldn't know when I got started and when I didn't, so sometimes I got an early start.

Looking back on it, having me, a drunk and a grown man, sneaking around their house had to be awful. But very little, if anything, was said about my drinking. At bare minimum, I did try to keep their house clean and I even cooked a meal from time to time.

As far as my plan to move out and get back on my feet, I continued to make phone call after phone call, reaching out to business owners about upgrading to the financial management software I was offering. I just kept "dialing for dollars," hoping for that perfect phone call that would bring in the big bucks.

Relationship building, educating potential clients, and selling proved to be incredibly and painstakingly slow, but I kept at it. I knew I had a great product and service to offer, but getting a client one at a time was going to take forever to build a residual income at a level to support myself. The residual income was one of the most appealing parts of the slow growth, however. Residuals meant I would earn money on each client account for the life of the account. Rather than just making one commission per sale, I would actually make money for as long as they used the product! I compare this type of income to running a marathon, as opposed to a sprint. The commissions are small and take time to build. However, my patience for slow-moving was running out!

I began reaching out to my previous employer...the seminar company. I just knew if they would have me back, I could support myself and live in hotels across the country and things would get back to normal. Or better yet, if I could get them to incorporate this product into their seminars, we could all make a lot of money...quickly. I had already adapted my sales pitch to those in the medical, dental, and chiropractic fields, and I could see how easily the seminar company could build this into their presentation.

Each time I called and spoke with my previous supervisor, he made promises to bring me back at some point, when the timing was right for both of us. Later, I would find out why he needed a few more months...he bought out the company's owner. Once I knew that, I was willing to hold on. At times, the bourbon would lower my inhibitions and I'd explain the timing couldn't be more right for me...I was homeless, needed money, and had a desire to get my life on track. Yep, I literally told him that during a phone call or two, and can you believe just over a year later, he would actually hire me on again? Although he'd hire two people before he ultimately had me back, my persistence paid off and I'd eventually get back to leading seminars.

In the seminar business, a person gets to tell their story or intertwine a sales pitch to a room full of potential buyers. It really doesn't matter what the story or pitch is, so long as the group is compelled to take action. I really focused on this type of "sell" and tried to relate it to my current situation of calling one business at a time. One day, a light bulb clicked on in my brain. I began calling individual companies who already had a client-base that could use my product. I began focusing on affiliate marketing to bring in several clients at a time vs. one or two here and there. This way, a company who had 100 (or more) satisfied clients could recommend my services and earn a little bit for themselves by recommending it. Although still a slow process in gaining consistent income, I could see the writing on the wall. I was on my way to building a residual income I'd be able to live on.

I worked from "home" in Indianapolis making phone calls, drank bourbon for the better part of 12 hours a day, and tried to be on my *best behavior* so as not to upset anyone at the house in Indy. The couple I stayed with were beyond awesome. I was inspired by their generosity, money management, and commitment to their *fellow man* – not just to me, but everyone. Another thing that couple did for me was to cover me; not just covering my drinking problem, but the very fact I was staying in their home was kept out of conversations they had with friends, family, and social media.

Within a few months of staying with them, my income (all of about $300 to $400 per month) was becoming steady. Still poor and unable to afford my own housing, but thankfully no longer constrained to a $10 weekly food budget. Things were heading in the right direction. My shame and self-disappointment was lessening, but still prevalent.

11

Running Scared

2009 (Indianapolis)

A whole year flew by and I couldn't believe I was still in Indianapolis. I had big plans and *needed* to get back to the West Coast. The shame and emptiness that still lived in me was exhausting, but at least I was no longer suffering with depression. I just had to keep doing what I was doing, and I knew things would right themselves. After all, I had quite the story to tell now. All of this would mean *something*, someday. Yes, this story of my real-life struggles and heartache (plus how my committed friends and family supported me along the way which allowed me to rebound) *would* make a difference in other people's lives. I knew that whenever that *someday* came, and I was able to create ifinallyquit.com, somehow people would connect to my story of *overcoming*. I just hadn't overcome *yet*.

The calls to my previous employer continued. I kept pitching him on including the financial management software that I was selling to medical offices into in the seminar. It was one of those rare moments in business when you have the perfect product from one company and the perfect delivery method with another. These discussions continued and seemed like we were on the cusp of making us all a lot of money. If ever there was a win-win-win-win solution all around...this was it. The financial management software company would win. The seminar business owner would win. The attendees of the seminar would win. And, I would win. What could go wrong? Nothing…other than the owner of the seminar company was greedy to the point of doing nothing. I certainly didn't know it at the time, but he didn't move forward on this opportunity because he didn't want to equally share the profits. He didn't want to share the revenue with me, the drunk who brought this to his attention. The really unfortunate part of not getting this deal put together was not knowing why until three years later. At this point though, in mid-2009, he was ready to get me back on the road on a "trial basis" to see if I could still do the job.

There were challenges to getting back on the road and navigating across the country; some challenges the employer and I expected, and some that came out of nowhere. As I address a couple of them, one thing of note here is that two years had gone by without me having a cigarette. I continued to be thankful that I was no longer chained to smoking or sought out cigarettes in times of stress. Believe me, I had more than a few stressful moments in that time! I was renewed every day I went without a cigarette or thinking about them.

Honestly, the most I thought about smoking was trying to figure out how to build a community of people who wanted to join me in not smoking. The dream of I Finally Quit, Inc. was always in the back of my mind. But for now, I had to focus on the seminar business and getting from point A to point B without a credit card for car rentals or money for plane tickets and food while travelling. The seminar company no longer utilized corporate credit cards or gave a cash advance for incidentals on the road. There were a lot of hoops to jump through and exceptions to be made in getting me back out on the road. Although these "obstacles" were overcome one at a time, a major one was still lurking that only my consumption of alcohol seemed to help.

11

Running Scared

2009 (Indianapolis)

A whole year flew by and I couldn't believe I was still in Indianapolis. I had big plans and *needed* to get back to the West Coast. The shame and emptiness that still lived in me was exhausting, but at least I was no longer suffering with depression. I just had to keep doing what I was doing, and I knew things would right themselves. After all, I had quite the story to tell now. All of this would mean *something*, someday. Yes, this story of my real-life struggles and heartache (plus how my committed friends and family supported me along the way which allowed me to rebound) *would* make a difference in other people's lives. I knew that whenever that *someday* came, and I was able to create ifinallyquit.com, somehow people would connect to my story of *overcoming*. I just hadn't overcome *yet*.

The calls to my previous employer continued. I kept pitching him on including the financial management software that I was selling to medical offices into in the seminar. It was one of those rare moments in business when you have the perfect product from one company and the perfect delivery method with another. These discussions continued and seemed like we were on the cusp of making us all a lot of money. If ever there was a win-win-win-win solution all around...this was it. The financial management software company would win. The seminar business owner would win. The attendees of the seminar would win. And, I would win. What could go wrong? Nothing...other than the owner of the seminar company was greedy to the point of doing nothing. I certainly didn't know it at the time, but he didn't move forward on this opportunity because he didn't want to equally share the profits. He didn't want to share the revenue with me, the drunk who brought this to his attention. The really unfortunate part of not getting this deal put together was not knowing why until three years later. At this point though, in mid-2009, he was ready to get me back on the road on a "trial basis" to see if I could still do the job.

There were challenges to getting back on the road and navigating across the country; some challenges the employer and I expected, and some that came out of nowhere. As I address a couple of them, one thing of note here is that two years had gone by without me having a cigarette. I continued to be thankful that I was no longer chained to smoking or sought out cigarettes in times of stress. Believe me, I had more than a few stressful moments in that time! I was renewed every day I went without a cigarette or thinking about them.

Honestly, the most I thought about smoking was trying to figure out how to build a community of people who wanted to join me in not smoking. The dream of I Finally Quit, Inc. was always in the back of my mind. But for now, I had to focus on the seminar business and getting from point A to point B without a credit card for car rentals or money for plane tickets and food while travelling. The seminar company no longer utilized corporate credit cards or gave a cash advance for incidentals on the road. There were a lot of hoops to jump through and exceptions to be made in getting me back out on the road. Although these "obstacles" were overcome one at a time, a major one was still lurking that only my consumption of alcohol seemed to help.

In the beginning of this trial re-employment, we decided to bypass the hassles of plane tickets and car rentals in other states by keeping me local for the first few tours. So, when there were tours in the Midwest, within driving distance of Indiana, I could rent a car with an Indiana driver's license and not have to worry about renting a car without a credit card, as debit cards were accepted for local drivers. Problem solved...right? Not exactly.

First, without being able to fly and rent cars, my income opportunities would be limited by the schedule. Secondly, something had been growing deep in my psyche over the last few years that I didn't even know about, until it was time to get back on the road. It must have stemmed from the failure I felt. For the most part, I had kept that failure bottled up inside. But now, it bubbled its way to the surface and I had a major problem on my hands. I was afraid! Afraid...of what?! *Everything!*

> **Fear debilitated me, gripping every part of my existence.**

It became apparent as soon as I got behind the wheel of the first rental car. It had been years since I drove on a highway at 60+ miles an hour. It wasn't just the speed or being behind the wheel. Fear gripped every part of my existence, even just being outside and seeing the vastness of the open road, the air, and the distance I had to travel. I was scared of everything.

Even now as I tell this part of the story, it's difficult to express just how debilitating and unforeseen this fear was. I was consumed by it. My heart would race out of my chest. I wanted to get out of the moving vehicle and sprawl out and cling to the ground. My breathing became haphazard, which only fueled my brain and internal voice shouting that I was going to die.

This was a vicious circle. My internal voice would scare me to the point of causing my heart to race even faster. This irrational (and I knew it was irrational) thinking and behavior spread into every aspect of my day and night. My brain was in overdrive, and really the only way (at the time) I found to slow it down was to consume more bourbon.

Somehow I made it through the first tour back on the road. My performances and sales during the seminars were nowhere near what I knew I was capable of. The rust of being away certainly showed, but I knew I could convince the company to give me another chance. And, thankfully they would, the next time they had something scheduled in my part of the country. It was slow going, but promising, especially because the talks of bringing the software into the seminars continued. I could see the "light at the end of the tunnel," or so I thought.

For the next few months, I would continue to sneak around the house in Indianapolis, trying to avoid creaking floorboards, loud television after the couple had gone to bed, and the occasional stumbling into a wall. I just knew I was on the right path and would soon be able to sustain my own apartment and living expenses again.

12

Travelin' Man

2010 (Across the US)

The frequency of my travels really began to pick up again in 2010. Although at the beginning of the year I wasn't quite back to full time with the seminar company just yet, I was definitely getting out more and more. There was really a lot going on for me now. Things really started moving...although not all for the good. A positive change, though, came in my finances. Both companies I was working for began paying me a little more. Both jobs were 100% based on commissions, and the software company had that residual income tied to it, so my pay increased ever so slightly over the years.

Between working the seminar business, which entailed being in a different city every day, and wanting to continue to build the residuals of the second company, my time was becoming more and more limited. However, the time commitments I gave to both companies did not take away from my time for alcohol consumption. In fact, even though I was flying and driving across the country, my drinking was increasing. With a more steady income, I was no longer buying 1.75L bottles one at a time, but *by the case*. Each case contained six bottles that would probably fulfill a bars needs for a week serving their entire customer base. I was going through one of these cases in under two weeks all by myself.

I never really tried to hide my alcohol consumption. The volume and the rate at which I was drinking were definitely exposed to the couple I was staying with in Indianapolis. It was also getting more and more noticeable to the employees and owner of the local liquor store. If I were on the road for two to three weeks in a row, they would make comments when I did show up about being fully stocked for me. I remember it registering in my mind how the employees took notice when I came in, and how it was a little embarrassing. But, I think the thing that stands out the most for me was the look of disgust (and borderline horror) on the face of one liquor store employee when I answered his question regarding *"my friends and I"* really liking that particular brand of whiskey. I had responded (without thinking) that *it was just me* drinking that whiskey. I wondered how many *regulars* they must have and how often the others in the neighborhood must frequent that place, and it was *me* who changed their ordering frequency. On one hand it was nice to be recognized, but on the other, having an impact on the local liquor store's business operations is nothing to be proud of.

The first few months of 2010 proved to be good for me financially, so I felt it was finally time to move out. This would also give my friends in Indianapolis a much needed reprieve from me staying at their place. I reached out to family in southern California, and asked if I could stay with them on the weekends, as I'd be flying in and out every week, and should be fairly unnoticeable. My dad and his wife were kind enough to invite me in with the understanding I'd have to find my own place relatively quickly, but they agreed it would be fun to have me around for a while.

It was great to have a change of scenery. Like many other places I'd stayed over the past four years, it didn't take me long to annoy and disrupt the routine of my hosts. It was the little things, too; things that I just didn't think about. For example, I liked to drink my whiskey on the rocks. To me, the sound of ice dropping into an empty glass triggered a "reward" feeling in my ears and mind…but to others, the sound of the ice dumping into the glass was a nearly constant (did I mention I was consuming a lot of booze?), annoying reminder that someone was occupying their space. I was somewhat cognizant of the "little things" and always tried to be a good houseguest, especially when at my lowest, financially. I cleaned up after myself and others, but at the end of the day, I was still infringing on someone else's life.

Trying to limit the amount of time I spent in someone else's home while flying in and out of southern California, I'd try to make plans to be gone on the weekends, too. I began staying over in the cities I was finishing a seminar tour in. Instead of rushing off to the airport on Friday afternoons, I'd take my time and stay the weekend at the host hotel. It made it easier on me and everyone else in my life at the time. People didn't have to make sure I was taken care of, and they didn't need to be home to entertain me. People didn't have to get to the airport to drop me off or pick me up. My life was really getting a little… simpler. In all candidness, not rushing off to the airport on Fridays really benefitted *me* the most.

At the end of each week, I now had the opportunity to take my time packing things up after the four-hour seminar. I could actually walk up to my hotel room, pour a drink, put my feet up for a bit, and then go back down in the early afternoon to ship materials back to the company. What it mostly allowed was more drinks, more often. Life seemed…easier.

I wasn't always able to stay over in the host city every Friday, so I did find myself back at my family's place a little more often than they may have liked. But again, I tried to be scarce. Well, things boiled over one weekend, and my dad's wife said something to me that jarred me to my core. Not enough for me to put the bottle down for good at that point, or even slow down my drinking, but it should have. I was, after all, still on a mission to drink a fifth of bourbon every day. I felt a compulsion to do it. I knew it would someday inspire others to quit drinking, so I pressed on and continued to drink. But that weekend afternoon, when I was called out to *be the man I was supposed to be*, something did change. I got in a taxi and disappeared for a few days to Los Angeles.

> "David, be the man you're supposed to be!"

As I sat and took inventory of my life, another panic attack kicked in and was consuming me. I laid down, pressing myself into the ground, and I swear I could feel the spinning of the earth. My mind was racing and had me convinced I'd be spun right off the face of the planet and off into space where I'd suffocate. These were real thoughts, and the fear I mentioned earlier was getting worse. I wasn't just afraid to drive or (God help me) drive over bridges, or of being a passenger in a car: I was afraid of…everything, at all times. I felt so insignificant, and if I were wiped from the face of the planet, would anyone even know? I had to make an impact or at least try. I didn't know how to build ifinallyquit.com or how I would write a book, but I knew I wanted to, not for me, but for those who want or need to quit…something.

As my mind raced, I could hear her strong words repeating in my head for the next few days; to *be the man I was supposed to be*. Things started to take shape. I didn't quite have a full-blown, fool-proof plan, but the outline of one was coming together. If I was going to help people and show them how to quit actions and behaviors that held them back, I'd most certainly have to do the same for myself. Although I was committed to consuming bourbon for the next couple of years, I was ready to change *the way* I was living. I just needed a safe place to stay, while I figured out what that meant. For the next couple of months, I stayed over at hotels across the country when I wasn't working, but it turned out I needed just a little more stability than that, so I reached out to my friends in Indianapolis again. After just a little bit of convincing, they opened their home up to me once more. This time with a commitment to pay rent and have an "exit strategy" built into our agreement.

This stay in Indianapolis would not last nearly as long as my last one. Being comfortable with my surroundings or appreciating the hospitality of my friends had nothing to do with the brevity of this stay: it was my alcohol consumption. I'm no longer using the word *consumption* as a word to mean the "act of drinking," but more of the old-school definition having to do with the *wasting away* of my body. Keeping the pace of 17 drinks a day was wreaking havoc to my physical and mental state. Through this decay, somehow I was able to get around the country without going to jail or injuring anyone. Somehow, I was able to continue to grow my residual income and strike partnership and affiliate deals with other software vendors, who added to my bottom-line. Somehow, I was able to meet the demands of travelling to a different city every day, while working.

God definitely had His hand on my life and protected me. There is simply no other explanation. Part of His plan was to continue to have people in my life who could facilitate my endeavors across the country and I needed help now…more than ever.

The fear I've mentioned a few times was now eating away at me nearly every moment of every day. I kept this to myself, but it was getting harder and harder to do so, as the fear I couldn't share with people now caused me to shake. Whether I was "home" in Indianapolis or travelling across the country, I could barely drive from point A to point B anymore. I was afraid to be in a hotel above the second floor. I couldn't present my seminar in rooms with windows or views of downtown metropolitan areas, nor could I present in a room *without* windows, especially if the door to the room was closed. Fear was debilitating and threatening my comeback, if you could call it that. I needed help and I needed it right away.

Over the course of a few months, I tried hypnosis…twice, with two different hypnotists. To have myself (or worse, someone else) poking around in my brain scared me so much I couldn't relax enough to have the hypnosis be of any help. Something had to give. Enter my bright idea of reaching out to former acquaintances from years past: other drinkers and misfits (I use the term lovingly). Instead of facing my fears head-on and stopping this slow-motion train-wreck of a life I was living and putting the bottle down, I began flying people into the cities where I was working, so I'd have "a driver" to get me around. Enter my first assistant.

Adding the expense of a second person on the road was something I'd never been able to do in the past and definitely not the best idea at this particular point. If my *master plan* was to get healthy and have my own place to live, supporting someone else on the road would prove to be a significant roadblock. In my own arrogance, I pressed on thinking I'd come up with the right way to get this all accomplished. And so it went for the remainder of the year and through the winter of 2011. I'd sparingly fly in and out of Indianapolis, staying in the cities where my seminars were on Fridays, when possible. I just had to manage flying someone else in and out of wherever I was.

After all the years of wanting to get back to the seminar life, all the wasted time getting to, navigating through, and waiting at airports was taking its toll on me, physically and mentally. I decided to search online for a place to stay in the "hub" city of my preferred airline at the time. What transpired over the next couple of months will have you saying, "No way!" out loud… again.

13

Must Have Gotten Lost

2011 (Indianapolis to Phoenix)

In April of 2011, I came to the conclusion that the time I spent travelling or making sure I was in the right place to be able to travel was consuming way too much of my time. Travelling for a living sounds like such an awesome experience to those who do not do it on a weekly or even monthly basis. It is exhausting. Consider needing to catch a flight from the eastern US time zone between the hours of 6:30 am to 9:00 am on a Monday morning. For me, I needed to wake around 4:30 am to make sure I was showered and ready to go, and there were numerous times I didn't fall asleep (after drinking all day) until 1:00 am, so I'd be operating on very little sleep. I'd need to call and wait for a taxi to take me to the airport.

Once at the airport, being a "super elite" traveler does have a few perks though, so time wasted by standing in lines is dramatically reduced. However, there are still the check-in and security processes to go through. By now, I had figured out how to travel with bourbon on me and in my carry-ons, so there was one line I didn't mind standing in: the one at the airport coffee shop to get a to-go cup with ice.

I'd lose more time flying from Indianapolis to a "hub" city for whichever airline I was flying, so that typically meant 2.5-3 hours to get to Phoenix or Philadelphia, just to board another 3+ hour flight to get to my true destination. The turnaround on Friday usually meant another 12 hours or so of wasted time. To counteract that and eliminate it entirely, and living out of suitcases for the most part by now, I decided to move to a hub city and do away with two entire legs of travel every week. Seems reasonable…right?

I reached out to a friend who lived in Phoenix, and got her opinion on the city and if she felt it would be a good place for me. In spite of her repeated warnings about the extreme temperatures, I decided I was ready to make the move. Other than her, I didn't know anyone in Phoenix, so I decided to check out a few websites that put potential roommates together or had information about inexpensive places near the airport. I didn't really want the expense of my own apartment, even though I probably (finally) could have afforded one at this time, so I found a guy renting a room via a website that offered a myriad of services. Later, I'd wish I would have chosen a website specifically for finding roommates, as it would have really limited the stress and disgust that was awaiting me.

Upon arriving in Phoenix to meet my new roommate, who'd made a commitment to get me to and from the airport whenever needed, I was looking forward to settling into a lifestyle that was going to limit the amount of time spent in airports. True to his word, he was there to get me right on time. The room I was renting from him was actually located at an apartment complex, not in a residential home. Not knowing the city of Phoenix, I didn't know whether I was in a "good" part or "bad" part of town prior to my arrival at the complex, but it quickly became apparent there were definitely nicer parts of town than where I was. But, it was okay. I really just needed a place on a couple of weekends here and there. The first night came and went without incident. My friend who lived in town came to pick me up in the morning so I could get some necessities for my new room.

She was not overly impressed with the location, but I let her know I'd make the most of it. Now, this is going to sound strange to some readers, however, I was really making progress in life and it was the "little things" that let me know it. Sure, I was going to be paying rent for use of the room, but it was the bed sheets, shower curtain, towels, and other things I bought that allowed me to feel as if I were re-entering society. No more sleeping on floors or using other people's sheets or seeing *their* colors, but I got to hand pick my colors. I was excited to decorate *my* bathroom and room. This was the first time in nearly five years I owned something other than the clothes on my back and a bottle or two of bourbon. Compared to the way I had been living, this honestly felt like progress. *Were things finally moving in the right direction...for real?*

After taking the weekend to get re-acquainted with my friend, getting to know my new roommate, and feeling accomplished, it was time to get back to the airport and begin my *new* travels.

Travel was going to be so much easier, as everything and everywhere became connected with direct flights. There were no more plane changes and far fewer chances of delays. After flying in and out of Phoenix a couple of times, over the first month, I was really feeling great about my decision to relocate. The only challenge for me at the time was the temperature of Phoenix. Not even into the "dog days" of summer yet, and it was over 100 degrees nearly every time I flew in or out of the city, regardless of time of day. It was common for triple digit temperatures even after 10:00 pm. I could only imagine how scorching July and August would be. If you recall the timeline of the beginning of the book, you'll know the temperature was going to be the least of my worries in a couple of months. However, what happened next was shocking.

My first trip out of Phoenix actually lasted two back-to-back weeks followed by a quick weekend turnaround. So, my new roommate truly had hit the roommate *jackpot*, had one existed. True to my word, I would not be around very often, so he wouldn't necessarily have to change his day to day routine. Coming to the end of the first month of me paying rent in Phoenix, my roommate let me know in addition to his day job, he was also a part-time photographer and had an upcoming shoot that may take place over the next weekend. He let me know the "models" may need a place to stay during the photo-shoot, so he asked if I would mind staying in a hotel that he'd pay for during the next weekend and the models would stay at the apartment. Wanting to be cooperative, I let him know I would do it this one time, but in the future he should consider putting the models up at the hotel – not just for my convenience, but to create a comfortable and more professional setting for his models. (I truly was oblivious at times.)

That Friday, when I flew back into Phoenix, he picked me up at the airport then dropped me off at a local hotel, per our agreement. The next morning, when he picked me up at the hotel, he was noticeably perturbed. As we walked through the lobby, he let me know the models were in the car and would be joining us for breakfast. *Models AND breakfast*, I thought, *now this is living!*

It's not always the easiest to judge people's weight, height, or age, but we sure can get a general idea of those things by looking at one another. I say that because, upon exiting the car at the fast food restaurant for breakfast and seeing the models get out of the back of the car, I felt (instantly) these young ladies were…well, much too young. When the roommate instructed the three young ladies they could each order two things from the dollar menu, I really became disgusted and began working on an exit strategy.

Dropping me off at the apartment, the roommate and models left to take care of who knows what. I was completely mystified and in no way in denial, as I made my way up the three flights of stairs on the outside of the apartment building. Whatever was going on, I wanted nothing to do with it. Still wondering what the age of those young ladies really was, I entered the apartment to an absolute mess. There were drinking glasses and dirty dishes strewn throughout the apartment, complete with spilled vodka and cranberry juice all over the kitchen counter.

> Whatever was going on, I wanted nothing to do with it.

Having thrown a party or two in my college days, I had a pretty good idea of what took place here the night before. One thing I *was* sure of, *none* of those young ladies were old enough to be drinking alcohol! As I entered "my" room, it was evident my bed had been slept in, my bathroom was a mess, and there was even the remnants of a spilled cocktail all over my new sheets.

Later that afternoon, when the roommate returned, I nonchalantly brought up the age of the "models" with him. I remember shuddering at how this man in his mid to late 50's told a very vivid story of how he had waited four years to photograph these 15-year-old girls. He was also very upset that his "shoot didn't go the way he wanted it to." You know how you just get a feel for a situation and know you want nothing to do with it? That's where I was...no longer wanting anything to do with being under the same roof as this man.

I had my friend come pick me up. As I told her of the events that transpired, we came to the conclusion that if I felt like what was happening *was* happening, it would be best for me to get out of that living situation as quickly as possible. Not wanting to put myself in jeopardy or have anything to do with contributing to the delinquency of minors or something even worse yet, I decided to sleep over at my friend's house that night. We both agreed, I'd worked way too hard for way too long to have everything taken away from me (again), but this time for no reason other than answering a website ad for a roommate.

Having a conversation about how best to get my things out of this man's apartment, we came to the conclusion I could keep my belongings at her place for the next couple of weeks as I flew in and out for work. We had an understanding that on the next full weekend I was in Phoenix, she and I would look for an apartment for me, as neither one of us really saw the benefit of me staying indefinitely at her home.

The next afternoon, we went back to the apartment to collect my belongings. We didn't see the roommate's car when we arrived, so we were both relieved thinking we could get my things out of there quickly and without any uncomfortable conversations about why I was suddenly leaving. We moved at such a hurried pace, grabbing clothes, sheets, and bathroom supplies by the armful and moving them down the three flights of stairs, taking the stairs two at a time and heading back up for the next round. It was July and 110 degrees outside. Between the temperature, my blood alcohol level, and clearing out the room in under an hour, I was feeling nauseous and lightheaded from moving so fast. On the last trip inside to get the last few remaining items, the roommate's bedroom door opened.

We were not prepared for the awkwardness of the situation that was about to unfold. It was now around three in the afternoon and the roommate stumbled out, disheveled, hair a mess, and bathrobe unbound. He fidgeted getting himself covered, then reached toward my friend to give her a handshake. His offer was declined and he asked what we were up to for the rest of the day. It quickly became apparent he had no idea we just packed up my things as if a flood were on its way. I made up a quick story *on the fly* about how now that my friend and I were living in the same city, we thought we'd make a go of a relationship, so we were moving in together. There was no need to really build too much of a back story to this, so I left him a couple of hundred dollars for partial rent and let him know I was moving out.

My friend and I removed ourselves from the apartment and never looked back. Later that evening, I called the local police to let them know of my suspicions and what I had witnessed over the weekend. I'm not sure whatever came of it, but I was relieved to be out of there…and just like that, I found myself needing to find a place to live…once again.

14

All I Ever Wanted Was a Place to Call My Own

August 6, 2011 (Scottsdale)

Two weeks later I returned to Phoenix, after another whirlwind tour with nine stops across two states. My friend and I set out looking for my new apartment. This was such a huge step for me. This time, there would be no room to rent. I wanted my own place. We were looking in the Scottsdale area, which is a little pricey, but convenient to the airport and had many local restaurants and bars. It reminded me a bit of downtown San Diego. I'd be able to walk to bars and stumble home, which was a big selling point for me.

Other than the incessant heat (it was common for the high temperature to be over 115 degrees through the summer), I was looking forward to all of the possibilities and adventures that awaited me. By 11:00 am, we'd already checked out a couple of complexes and were touring the third. It was during this tour that I was confronted for the first time about one of my biggest kept secrets. As I was drinking my "coffee" and walking the grounds of the apartment complex, my friend asked if there was truly coffee in the cup or if it was something else. I had no problem letting her know it was bourbon. She had a big problem with it.

The time of day bothered her, because she quickly figured out there hadn't been coffee at all in that cup I'd been carrying around all morning. She shared her opinion of drinking that much bourbon in the morning, and how I needed to get a grip on reality. Her main focus turned to my disrespect of her and my lack of responsibility for my actions. She was upset that she was driving around the Phoenix area with someone who had an open alcohol container. She explained that had any little thing gone wrong with her car or had we been pulled over for any reason, there would be consequences to *her*. Once again, I realized I'd put my needs and desires before someone else's, but had little regard for her feelings. I threw out the remainder of the drink, and with little to no embarrassment, rode to the next appointment, which turned out to be the "perfect" location for me...or so we thought.

> Once again I had put my desires before someone else's needs and feelings.

This place had it all...prestige, location, amenities, new construction, vaulted ceilings, a couple of swimming pools on the grounds, and much, much more. More importantly, it was close to many bars. I was excited and quite honestly a little nervous about filling out the application. After all, I'd been homeless and completely *off the grid* for half a decade. When it came to maintaining a credit history, I hadn't. After losing my condo just five years ago, I really hadn't paid any of my financial obligations. Amazingly, the management of the apartment complex in Scottsdale was willing to look the other way because of my current monthly income, which was now more than $7,000 a month.

They accepted my application and I was scheduled to move in

on the first of September. *Phew…what a ride*, I remember thinking at the time. Five years of struggle, living hand-to-mouth, a journey that traversed the entire width of the United States from California to Florida and stops in between, with lows of sleeping overnight in a park, losing the respect of friends and peers, getting fired after securing the "perfect job," travelling the world, and being in the worst physical shape of my life. Then to the highs of quitting cigarettes, bonding with family, building two income streams, and finally securing my own place to live again.

The craziness seemed to be behind me. I was sure I'd never forget the summer of 2011. This was the first time in years my confidence level was on the rise. I certainly wasn't expecting to end up in the hospital just a couple of days later. I really didn't think I was prepared to be uprooted again, but this time, I'd make sure it was the last. I knew all the highs and lows of my story would encourage and inspire others. This time…I'd change the world!

15

Ain't it the Truth

August 8, 2011

Back to the beginning of this story: the fateful day of the bad burrito, the blue cocktail, the pain, the need to get to San Francisco and not strand my assistant there...the day I would miraculously make it to the emergency department before my body shut down. After all the tests, procedures, and results, I am taken to the Intensive Care Unit.

San Francisco ICU

In the days that followed my admittance to the ICU, I would slip in and out of consciousness as the medical staff adjusted pain medications and monitored my failing pancreas and liver. My kidneys weren't doing so well either. I was truly in a fight for my life. However, it wasn't really *me* that was fighting. This would be the direst of situations, as my life as I knew it on this planet could end at any given second, but there wasn't really a "*me*" there. I had *checked out*. I wish I had a gallant story about how I knew I was fighting and I was grinding out victory after victory, but the fact was my mind wasn't there, and my body was on auto-pilot.

Once in the ICU, there wasn't much for me to do at all. The

medical staff monitored my every breath, pulse, and enzyme level. They did all they could do to alleviate and manage the pain. Come to find out, the only way to treat my overworked and ill-functioning pancreas was to allow it to "reboot" or reset itself. That meant it needed a complete and total break from the digestive process – no food, no water, no ice chips, no sustenance, whatsoever. For the next 8 days, nothing would enter my body other than IV fluids (with no nutritional value) and pain medication. That was it! And, for the first time in years, there was an 8-day stretch where no booze entered my body. If you are wondering about weight loss and if this is an effective way to go about it, well…yes, there was weight loss (27 pounds in two weeks), but no, this is certainly *not* the way to go about it.

In order to control the pain, I was given morphine and other pain medications. With pain medications at high levels, I had to be closely monitored and woken every couple of hours. The ICU staff seemed to be continually asking me if I knew the date or where I was. I'm pretty sure I answered their questions

> **My body had not known this level of relaxation in a long time…**

correctly or at least to the best of my ability. One thing I knew for sure was that the pain went away completely every couple of hours, and my body and mind had not known this level of relaxation in a long time. Every couple of hours, I'd become aware of the pain, but with the next influx of morphine, it was gone again. I truly was unaware that I was actually nodding in and out of reality. These medications were actually causing some vivid hallucinations. At one point, I'd hallucinated myself into a couple of popular television shows and the ICU staff into supporting characters.

Over the course of the next eight days, this was my life…no eating, no drinking and well…come to think of it, this really is no life at all. My "life" was really on pause and hung in the balance. Could the medical staff assist my body in recovering? There really wasn't much to do other than pass in and out of consciousness and deal with the pain while I was coherent. The pain was not just in my abdomen and failing organs, but there was the pain of embarrassment and what I perceived others to now *know* about me. My *secret* was out. It's amazing how powerful the brain really is, to go from hallucinations to the worry and guilt that I felt of what others thought of me.

Remember, I was completely cut off from the world during these eight days. There were no phone calls in or out by me. Sure, my voicemail was filling up, but that was mostly work contacts trying to find me, but certainly no conversations to be had. The ICU had tracked down my sister in Florida and my brother in Indiana. There were conversations about how to get my body out of the hospital, as no one was certain I would actually walk out of there.

I never hid from my brother or sister the actual amount I drank. When I was living in my brother's basement and sleeping on the floor of my sister's spare room, I had temporarily transferred my financial burden of purchasing alcohol to them. They knew the *amount*…what they now knew was the *damage* I'd inflicted upon myself. According to the doctors and the rest of the medical staff, the very next drink of alcohol I had was going to kill me. When the ICU staff put it in those terms to my family, they were horrified. They knew they had just received a "dead man walking" notice, because they all believed that I would not be able to quit drinking. They (unlike me) already knew my addiction and commitment to drinking surpassed everything else: my financial well-being, my fiancé, and even my self-worth.

Losing everything hadn't been enough for me to change my behaviors or remove the blinders from my eyes. Even laying in the ICU as my body was shutting down was not enough for me to get a grip. Fortunately for me, I didn't have much further to go to *rock bottom*. That would come in just a few days.

The phone calls from the medical team to my family were incredibly unfair to my brother and sister. They had witnessed the last 20 years of my life, and they *knew* how much I was drinking. They were scared for me and couldn't afford the cost of travel to be with me. They both thought I would die alone.

My father and his wife would receive the call next. They were informed that I was fighting for my life. At the time, I had no way of knowing the financial and emotional burden my hospital stay would cause them, but even in tight financial times, my father was able to book a flight in a few days. He arrived about a week into my stay in the ICU. The truth was that I might not survive, so there was no real reason to get there any sooner. I wouldn't have known he was there anyway, and if I died...why be there to watch that?

Ironically, during the first eight days, my body was improving. My pancreas, liver, and kidneys were finally getting the rest they so desperately needed. Without the bombardment of alcohol, there was healing taking place. My emotional and spiritual healing were not far behind. Those phases of recovery would begin when I was transferred out of the ICU.

Some find group settings of like-minded or like-"addicted" people to be very rewarding and conducive to mental and emotional recovery. At the time of my hospital stay, there were no other people for me to talk with or hear stories of healing addictions or other abuses. Once the cloud of constant pain medications were lessened, I would have to begin facing the mental and emotional sides of how I'd ended up at the hospital...alone. Coincidentally, I was transferred out of ICU and into an isolation room. However, somehow I knew that I was not totally alone.

I was transferred to the isolation room because of a nasty little bug...*C. difficile (C. diff)*. This is an opportunistic bacteria that actually kills more than 30,000 people in the US every year, most of whom pick up the bug while in the hospital. Apparently, I'd been carrying around this infection *before* I arrived, and no one really knew for sure how long I'd had it. Anyone in the medical profession can tell you, dealing with the intestinal symptoms of this bacteria is rather gross, so I'll just leave it at that. Not only would a nurse have to come in and give me the antibiotic Vancomycin every four to six hours, but I would continue this antibiotic for six weeks! I found out later Vancomycin is expensive and powerful, costs more than $500 per week, and only used in extreme, last-ditch circumstances. But, while by myself, the isolation room proved to have a reality and deep symbolism about it that I would stare down for the next few days.

Transferring rooms was all a blur, due to being kept heavily sedated. I do remember feeling some relief being out of the ICU, but watching the hospital staff have to put on gowns, gloves, masks, hats, and shoe coverings just to come into my room to talk with me, draw blood, change IV bags, and even bring me food was pretty embarrassing for me. I was so sick and toxic, people had to wear real-life barriers to keep themselves from me. But even with the shame and embarrassment of being so physically sick, fragile, and weak, I still had not reached *the bottom*. Here I was: over a week spent in the hospital, nearly dead, and I still had not accepted the full reality of my addiction.

The isolation room was such a great and much-needed metaphor for me. I started to think of being isolated in this room and the reality of not having anyone come visit me besides my dad. I got to thinking about who I could call and get some emotional support from. I wracked my brain. I went through all my "contacts," even looking at my ICE (in case of emergency) contact in my phone, yet there really was no one to reach out to. *How can this be? How can I not have anyone to call?*

This really got me thinking of the consequences of my actions and behaviors over the years. *Is this really all there is to my life...bottles of bourbon as I traveled across the US, and no one to share my experiences with? Is this really who I am?* I wondered.

> Is this all there is to my life? Bourbon? But no real relationships?

I wish I could tell you this was the breakthrough moment for me, but I wasn't quite there yet. But, it was coming soon like a freight train. Five years in the making, my *rock bottom* was around the next turn. Unfortunately for me, I couldn't hear the train coming, and it was about to hit me square on, snapping me fully into reality – something I hadn't really faced due to my lack of sobriety. At this time, I didn't know I was using the booze to not *feel* the consequences I had created.

I really took some time to ponder how a *motivational* seminar leader who had presented to 20,000 people over a decade could have no real contacts. I didn't even have social media accounts. What huge opportunities I had missed in life. At this point, I wish I could tell you the sky rumbled and the seas parted and God Himself walked into the room to slap me around a bit, but that is not what happened. The freight train of truth actually started with a couple of subtle conversations I overheard happening out in the hallway, where some nurses were making plans for the upcoming weekend. It was kind of like being knocked over by a feather.

I will tell you exactly what I overheard and ultimately how, as a *giver*, I thought my action and behavior towards their conversation was absolutely normal. I'll set up the scenario, so you can *see* the absurdity of where I had steered my life.

Prior to being admitted to the ICU, I weighed 235 pounds. That may sound heavy, but at 6'-6" that was not too terrible... especially because I harbored the misguided thought that I fell into the "tall, dark, and handsome" category of men. I'd ultimately find out I was pretty delusional about that, as well. During the course of the eight days in ICU, I began to lose weight at a very rapid pace (under 24/7 care and monitoring by the doctors and nurses). Although I would start eating on day nine of my hospitalization, I would ultimately leave the hospital at just 208 pounds: 27 pounds lighter. For those of you thinking you could stand to lose a few pounds, I can guarantee you...acute pancreatitis and a *C. diff* infection is NOT the way you'd want to do it.

What's important to know about my rapid weight loss is it caused me to become very weak. In order to protect me from falling in this debilitated state, the hospital staff had a few options. Hospital beds have rails that can be moved up or down to prevent one from rolling out of bed, and these rails also make it extremely difficult for a patient to just spring to their feet due to the lack of a clear path. In extreme situations, hospital staff may physically restrain a patient with straps and tie-downs at their wrists to prevent them from getting up and falling. In my particular case, I was not tied down, although the staff threatened that as an option. They did keep my rails up, slowing my progress from getting up, but they had also come up with a clever notification system I was not aware of.

Because of my weakened state, the staff did not want me getting out of bed on my own, especially not to walk across the room...not even to use the bathroom. They placed a weight-activated notification device under my mattress that was triggered each time my weight was removed from the bed.

Each time I tried to get up to use the restroom, they knew it immediately. What I really wanted to do was take a shower, since it had been nine or ten days of going without one. I didn't know every time I got up, this device would alert staff by playing carnival music in the hallway.

I remember finding it odd that every time I went to make a break for the restroom, a nurse would be at my door. They were suddenly there, attentive to my every need...other than the shower I so desperately wanted. In regards to that, the nurses would say it wasn't time yet...*maybe tomorrow*. Ugh, so gross!

The first few days out of the ICU were a little confusing, but the pain medication levels were being reduced, and day by day my head began to clear. My father arrived, but for the life of me, I couldn't comprehend why he had flown up to see me. I mean, I was just a little sick and staying in the hospital for a few days, right? While he was there, the full gravity of my health issues had still not sunk into my booze-soaked brain. I remember while he was there I was having the hardest time charging my phone. It was completely dead and I wanted to check in with my voicemail and look through my contacts to see who I could call. It took me two days to figure out how to use my phone charger. But once charged, I did not find anyone to call.

I had just a couple of voicemails though, one of which really stood out. It was from my sales director at the software company. The concern in his voice was eerie. He was one of the last people I talked to on the phone while I was still on the ground in Phoenix. His message was full of pauses, and obviously he was choosing his words carefully. His message said, "Hey, uh, Dave...I hope you're not dead. You didn't sound so good...the last time we talked. I haven't heard from you in days and...I'm not liking that your phone is turned off. Uh...call me..."

My father was there a few days and then went back home. We didn't talk much, as there really wasn't much to say. It was great to have him there though. After a couple of days, it became apparent I was physically on my way to recovering, so he went back home and I stayed to complete my care.

Within a couple of days, I was feeling better, and I really wanted to get cleaned up...but there was that carnival music again! Each time the staff was there to protect me from myself. But, with each passing day I was getting just a bit quicker, and then it happened...the moment that made me face the reality of so many bad decisions I'd made over the last decade. But, it didn't stop there...I could see the folly of my ways throughout most of my teenage and adult life. This type of reality and enlightenment was soul-crushing, and I'd have to truly face it...sober. The waves of reality were about to come pounding on me, over, and over, and over.

So, the conversation I mentioned overhearing was coming from the nurses in the hallway. They were talking about going out to some bars and dance clubs during the upcoming weekend. This wasn't just a couple of people getting together, but these nurses were planning a *party*. They were making plans to meet at one of their houses for cocktails before going out. I started to reminisce of times before I had become "homeless" or "without home"...*maybe that's a better way to say it*. As I thought back on having people come over to my place before we went out for the night, I remembered always having a fully stocked bar, some music playing, and we'd laugh and joke; we'd have fun. Something I had forgotten how to do over the years was to just have fun and enjoy life. As these nurses were making plans, I was thinking, *well, I may be in no shape to join in this party they're going to have this weekend, but I could still contribute.*

I always traveled with quite a lot of booze, remember? Well, I left a few details out. Not only did I travel with my 3 ounce liquids Ziploc bag full of miniature bottles, but I also traveled with a flask. Not just one flask, but a couple of flasks. And…not just the smaller ones that fit in a back pocket or inside a suit coat pocket (I had those too), but the larger ones that made transporting bourbon in my suitcases a little bit easier. As I thought of their party and the pre-party and the cocktails and the laughing and joking and the fun they were planning, I thought, *I should give them the bourbon in my suitcases.* Wait for it…so, I made a deliberate and concentrated effort to get out of bed! I'd walk over to the closet, get my suitcases out, and get out the flasks and bottles of bourbon to give to the nursing staff.

As I shakily stood to my feet (*there's that carnival music again*), I took a step, and then another. The male nurse with his British accent was telling me in a raised voice to get back in bed. As he clumsily fumbled with his gown, gloves, and shoe covers, I assured him it was going to be okay. This time I *was* getting out of this bed! *I just needed to get to my things.*

Luckily, he made it over to me before I collapsed. I hadn't been out of bed and on my own two feet in ten days. He tried getting me to turn around and head back to the bed, but I refused. I was going to make it to my suitcase. I kept assuring him it would be okay, as I had something to give to him. As he assisted me, I explained that I had heard of their upcoming party and I wanted to impart a gift upon them for taking such great care of me. He couldn't imagine what I could possibly have in my suitcase that would be so important to me to give to them.

We made it to my things, and as I proceeded to pull out flask after flask and bottle after bottle, the look of *horror* on his face was unmistakable. He knew instantly that if I had gotten my hands on *any* of this alcohol in any of the days or nights prior and drank even just a few ounces more, my pancreas and liver would have shut down for good, and I'd have been lying on the floor...dead! In combination with the look on his face and the stern reprimand I would receive from my doctor later that day, it sank in...I almost died from drinking alcohol. Not because of one night of overindulgence, but 25 years of constant and incessant alcohol abuse. Wait for it...remember me mentioning a freight train was coming? Well, it had been gaining momentum and I was on the tracks...on its way...and I had no idea...

And then, BAM! There it was...the moment of realization that the procurement, transportation, consumption, and cover up of booze *was* my entire life. I had pushed people and opportunity to the side to make sure I could get my hands on my next drink. The reality that I had put myself and my addiction above everything and everyone else was... crushing. I was a horrible, hurtful, self-indulgent, narcissistic asshole, and I'd completely failed as a human being. I was a horrible son to a mother who had since passed away, and a father who I don't have much in common with. I was a horrible sibling to my brother and sister, and had failed miserably at being the supporter I should have been.

The realizations kept coming. The metaphorical freight train had hit me...*I had nearly died just a few days ago. I was in the ICU for a week: the one place no one at the hospital wants a person to be, because their life is touch and go. I had no one to call to be near me in this time of need.* But...the reality was...I was STILL here.

> I came to the conclusion that I had put myself here. Booze had possessed me for so long.

It was like a 1,000 pound weight had just crushed my emotional and spiritual being, but just as quickly, I determined I would (metaphorically) rise up and take the responsibility for all of it. I came to the conclusion that I had put myself here, and I *could* get better and be better – as a person. Maybe my story *could* motivate and help others so they wouldn't end up in an ICU. Just maybe someone would be spared the physical pain of what I'd just gone through, not to mention the guilt and shame that came with the realization that an inanimate object (in this case booze) had possessed me for so long. My drinking caused me to make some highly questionable decisions before, but...*never again!*

One of the brightest silver linings was that I had already had the conversation with myself over the years about quitting drinking. After all, it really was my plan to quit drinking when I turned 40. Although incredibly ill-conceived, I did have a plan. It just so happened my body couldn't handle the nonstop consumption of alcohol and it shut down prior to the self-imposed deadline or *quit date*. Because I had quit smoking after being addicted to cigarettes for more than 20 years, I already knew I *could* quit whatever I put my mind to. I knew how to quit, and for me, quitting drinking was going to be a lot like quitting cigarettes.

But first, leading up to my discharge from the hospital, I took the time to ask myself and others some very tough questions. Of myself, I wanted to know things like, *could I be a better man, could I truly do a 180 and live my life without alcohol, could I get the help I needed, and would I allow that help to change my actions and behaviors that would lead to change of different consequences?* Because these thoughts and realizations were setting in (on top of knowing I was physically frail), the emotion of it all was just as devastating.

Over the next couple of days I would have very candid and open conversations with myself and counseling staff who would talk to me about addiction and rehab, as well as with the medical staff. All of the staff did a very good job of educating, informing, and warning me that the very next alcoholic drink (should I have one) could and would kill me. Together, we worked on a plan to help me make some very radical changes in my behavior.

We discussed "triggers" that could create situations that would lead to drinking. These triggers were loneliness (travelling all over the country and for the most part being alone while doing it), lack of stability (not having a home), and comfort (doing the same thing I had always done). I made the *mental* commitment to myself, but what about the *physical* triggers and reminders? And, *where* would the recovery take place?

> Triggers are situations that can lead to drinking, such as loneliness, lack of stability, and needing comfort.

According to the hospital staff and my own thinking, I needed stability and I needed it now. If I were to truly overcome my addiction and habit of drinking nearly all day long for over 20 years, it would take a radical change from how I had lived my life up to this point. The first thing that needed to change was establishing a place to lay my head at night. I needed a home. The newly signed lease in Scottsdale was not going to be the solution.

The counselor at the hospital also made it very clear that unless I was to physically check into a rehab facility, I would fail, and failure would lead to drinking that one last lethal drink. I finally agreed to check into a rehab center. The counselor went to work to find one that would allow me to check-in immediately upon my discharge from the hospital. My primary care physician was located in San Diego, so the counselor concentrated her efforts on rehab facilities there. I honestly felt relieved that the rehab center would be responsible for my sobriety and well-being, because I was already finding ways in my head to not take 100% responsibility for myself. The counselor convinced me that without the proper support offered by an in-patient facility, my chances of survival were almost non-existent. The sheer willpower to make the change on my own was something most people do not possess, she informed me. This line of (almost defeatist) thinking really made me hopeful and excited that programs like in-patient rehab existed. I'd be "sequestered" and unable to go purchase booze. *Sign me up, I'm ready*, I thought.

The next day the counselor returned to my room with good news! She had found a facility in San Diego that was part of my insurance plan. She let me know she'd already reached out to them and sent my files, along with her assessment. One of the biggest factors of getting in right away was my willingness and belief of my need for this rehabilitation. I was ecstatic about the possibilities, and knowing my insurance would help cover the cost of the recommended 30-day stay was a huge relief. My lead medical doctor in San Francisco was also excited. It really seemed to all of us we had done it: we found a fool-proof plan to get me the help I needed. Over the next few hours, I got in touch with the airlines and did one of the things I did so well – I booked a flight…destination San Diego – America's Finest City.

In just two short days, I'd be on my way. Mentally, I was feeling really good. The morphine and pain meds were just about cleared from my system, there was a plan in place for my continued recovery, and I *wanted* to be better. Physically, I could get out of bed on my own without that silly carnival music. Life was good…right? I took the final full day at the hospital to mentally prepare for the journey I was about to embark on. Not just the short, 90-minute flight to San Diego, but a life without booze. I relaxed and tried to really wrap my thoughts around what a life without booze would mean to me and what failure would also mean. Failure was NOT an option, but I did want to educate myself on all possible outcomes, so I wanted to talk to my lead doctor one more time before leaving the hospital at 4:00 am the next morning.

This doctor had overseen my entire stay. I had developed a lot of respect for her knowledge, compassion, and understanding of my situation. After a few minutes of expressing my gratitude, it was time for me to ask one question, one final time. The question had already been answered for me several times, but I just wanted my innermost consciousness, me at my core, to fully understand the answer. So, I asked again, "Doc, I understand my current physical state – my body is weak due to weight loss, my internal organs are severely damaged, and my mental health is pretty fragile, too. I get what's going on with me, and I fully understand how I got here. My question to you is…let's just say I don't make it to the rehab facility tomorrow for whatever reason. If I find myself at a bar with a glass of bourbon in front of me (I had no desire to drink, but…), yes, let's just say I end up in a bar with a drink. What would REALLY happen if I drank it down?"

> Mr. Ross, if you're somehow capable of getting another drink in you, you'll be dead before you hit the ground.

Her emotionless, icy, matter-of-fact answer was bone-chilling, and exactly what I needed to hear. She said, "Mr. Ross, if you are somehow capable of getting that drink in you…you'll be dead before you hit the ground." So, that was it! I was done.

The next morning, a great journey began. I would become "David the quitter." *I'd already quit smoking, how much harder could quitting drinking really be?* I thought, especially with a *life of luxury* in a rehab facility. Around 4:00 am, the nursing staff started prepping me for my discharge: IVs were coming out, I was allowed to shower on my own, my prescriptions were filled and placed in my bags, and a taxi was called to take me to the airport. Everyone agreed this was one of the stranger discharges they'd seen in quite some time.

The staff wheeled me out to the curb along with my two suitcases, both of which were carry-ons that I'd traveled with for years. Today, however, they were both just a bit lighter, as they were missing a combined two liters of bourbon. It felt as if 1,000 pounds had been removed from my baggage. The taxi driver asked several times if I was sure I was supposed to be going to the airport, because he had never picked someone up so weak and frail who was heading to an airport. He thought I might be "escaping" or signing out against medical advice. I assured him everything was legit, and off we went.

Truth be told, as I sat in the back of the taxi, I was confused, scared, and anxious. Traveling sober was going to be a whole new adventure, but then again…so was life. On the way to the airport, I soaked in as much of my surroundings as possible, gazing at the beautiful skyline of San Francisco. I felt every pothole on the freeway. I noticed the grayness of the sky turning to hues of orange as the sun was rising. In the back of my mind, I really wondered how the rehab facility was going to pan out. Would I "fit in" with other patients or would I be standoffish? What was life going to be like?

It was a quick ride to the airport, and I was already checking in for my 6:00 am flight. Walking up to and getting through security was a breeze this time. There would be no anxiety of expecting someone to discover my peculiar Ziploc bag of booze. And, the flight to San Diego was uneventful.

16

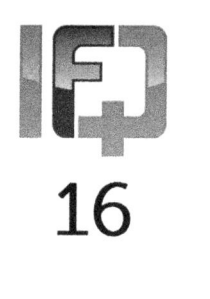

Recovery

August 23, 2011 (San Diego)
8:00 AM

Reality was lurking just around the corner to throw me several curveballs. The first was my colleague being late to pick me up from the airport. *Not that big of a deal, really. People run late, right?* Lateness and flakiness are actually two very big pet peeves of mine. I take things extremely personally, and feel these show no respect for another individual. But, I didn't want to put the energy into being upset. I had a long day in front of me. The last thing I wanted to do was get upset and cause myself to fail. And that was it...ultimately, it is ME who decides whether I fail or not...whether I drink or not...whether I live or not.

I was thankful we were only a tad bit delayed, because I REALLY had it in my head that I needed to get to this rehab facility immediately or I was going to die! I know I've stated that several times, but it's important to know just how powerful the mind is and what my thinking was at this time. *If I can just get admitted...I'll be okay.* I absolutely thought the ONLY way I would be able to avoid the inevitable cocktail was to get checked in as soon as possible. This way there would be no temptation and certainly no access to booze.

I fumbled with my bags, dragging them behind me. Of course there were wheels on the bags, but just walking a short distance was difficult. I was literally calculating in my mind how many more steps it would take to reach the sliding glass doors, how many more minutes until I could get checked in, and how long before I could just lay down. There was a huge relief and comfort upon entering the building. *I made it…everything was going to be okay.* However, this was not a 24-hour a day facility.

Curveball #2…We were there by 8:45 in the morning, but the doors were locked and there was no way to get in. Imagine our surprise. We saw a sign on the wall with the hours of operation posted, so we knew they'd be ready to go by 9:30. We decided to go get some breakfast.

On the way, we drove by a medical supply store and I quickly said, "Pull in here," in a raised voice. My colleague was a bit startled, but she made it into the parking lot. In my weakened state and remembering how winded I was just walking the 100 yards or so through the parking lot of the rehab center, I thought a cane would assist me. But, at my height one cannot just walk into one of these stores and buy the right size. They make them adjustable for people not quite as tall, or they make really tall canes that need to be custom cut. I didn't have time to wait 2-3 days to have it customized, so I purchased the tallest one and headed to Home Depot. Yep, the guys in the lumber department trimmed it down and we were good to go! Kind of comical, but I did leave there much more stable.

Next stop, breakfast. We had an open conversation about my health and who I was…a drinker. Although she had known me for almost ten years and knew me as a chronic drinker, we'd never talked like this. This was the same woman who opened her home to me before my time in Indiana. She knew my fiancé and had been there at the very beginning of me spiraling down. It was the very first place I stayed after losing my downtown condo five years prior.

I let her know I was in trouble…physically, mentally and emotionally. We talked about my plan to overcome alcohol. I preferred not to look at this as a setback or problem, but rather another chance at *winning* in life. I wanted to be known as the guy who overcame, not the guy who succumbed. As breakfast concluded, we headed over to the facility, where safety and comfort awaited.

Now that the facility was open, I was stunned to find out there was no counselor or psychologist on staff waiting at the front door for me and the front desk staff had no idea of who I was.

Curveball #3…They had no record of me checking in today. I was instantly pissed off and worried at the same time, mad that I'd made this journey and was not greeted with open arms, and worried about having nowhere else to go. Fear instantly set in. I had to get my emotions in check. Inside, I was a mess! In the past, these types of emotions and flying off the handle would cause me to reach for a smoke or a drink. Neither of those were an option anymore.

I had my discharge papers from the hospital, as well as notes from the psychologist from San Francisco. Now here was the *kicker*: the place I was at was NOT a rehab facility, but a mental health facility where "group meetings" were offered and counselors met one-on-one with people dealing with addiction. I wasn't at the wrong place…it just wasn't what the team in San Francisco and I were told it was. The front desk staff were looking at me like I was…well, crazy…as I informed them I was there to check in for 30 days. They could see I was in obvious need of…something, so they contacted their therapist who was taking emergency "walk-ins" that day. I was able to explain who I was and why I was there…to no avail. This day was certainly *not* going as planned.

As I showed the therapist my papers and explained my story of the last two weeks, he hung on my every word. I could tell he was intrigued and had compassion for me. As I wrapped up the story with the same words I'd been told by the counselor and doctors up north, I needed to be "admitted for 30 days or I was going to die," he could see my conviction and belief. The fact remained that this was not that type of facility, but he did know of some places. Although there was some relief in that, the trick was going to be getting into one of them.

I share the detail of trying to get into rehab, because of the expectation of the *sanctuary* I had built up in my mind. I believed this was going to be the ONLY way for me to survive. (Some of you reading this book may have similar feelings from time to time, as if there is only one option to take that leads to success and all others lead to doom.)

Well, it turns out…it wasn't the ONLY option. The self-responsibility and determination that would come from overcoming these initial curveballs would serve me incredibly well. The counselor's words in response to my recounting of the last few weeks was really jarring. He matter-of-factly informed me that this particular insurance carrier didn't just admit people into a rehab facility. Space was limited, and certain protocols and procedures had to be met prior to any referral to such a program. At this time, phone calls were made and the medical and counseling staff from the hospital did their best to try to get me into a facility, but the fact remained it just wasn't going to happen.

Now for any of you drinkers or smokers reading this, I'll let you know that my inner voice was screaming to give up. *Just get up, get out of here, and have a drink!* At any other time in life, I'd have listened.

> **My inner voice was screaming, "Just get up, get out of here, and have a drink!"**

But, something was different inside. If I did, I knew I'd let everyone down and disappoint myself, my family, acquaintances, and particularly the hospital staff who just saved my life. *I'd stay sober today*, I told myself. *There would be stressors in life, and I would have to deal with them differently than before.* I knew I'd have to react to things differently…change my previous actions and behaviors, if I truly wanted a different set of circumstances. The bottom-line was, I was not going to get into a facility today, and it would be up to me (and only me) to figure out something different.

I was informed that I could check into a private facility for thousands of dollars, but the fact remained, I had no *home base*, which meant nowhere to really go and think about or research private organizations. Maybe I had blinders on or maybe I should have got up and walked out, but confused, alone, and scared, I listened to the requirements for where I currently was. The whole process, including evaluations by the staff, attending group meetings, and attending introductory "addiction" education, would take seven to ten days…just to see if I would be a candidate for their program. With nowhere to stay, this was becoming more and more nerve-wracking. What I needed was somewhere to gather my thoughts, especially since the first *group* meeting wouldn't take place until the next morning.

I called a taxi and had them take me to a local hotel. I was now completely exhausted and sat down on the bed in my hotel room. The next thing I knew, I was waking up to find three hours had past. There I was…my first day out of the hospital with no supervision, and I wasn't in the one safe place I should have been; the one place where I wouldn't have unfettered access to booze. I wasn't in…rehab!

I turned on the television, and although I had no desire to get a drink, the temptation and onslaught of commercials touting the "awesomeness" of alcohol WAS there. I decided after being cooped up in the hospital for the last two weeks, I needed to get outside. The fresh air would be good for me. Now, how much temptation could there be in the Gaslamp District? Well, remember, the 60+ restaurants, bars, and liquor stores there? Did I want a drink? Truthfully…no, but the availability was there.

Later…much later…I would look back and see the triumph of that evening: not falling back into my normal ways. People would say I got off "easy" because I didn't have to deal with the physical detoxification process while in the ICU. That is such a defeated way of thinking. People like to think one person's way of quitting was easier than what they would go through…it's a coping mechanism. I totally get it, but what people forget is that our minds can *move* mountains (mine even landed a plane in Albuquerque once). When I was in the ICU, my body *did* go through detox, but my body was doing that every day before I ever was admitted to the ICU. Daily, my body would shake and tremble until I had a few drinks. Every day my bowels (septic from *C. difficile*) were twisted in knots or I faced the "urgency" of having to get to a bathroom (sorry to be so candid). Every day my body craved booze.

Here is my point…NOTHING at this time was easy. Physically, I *could* go get a drink…but it was the MENTAL strength that prevented it. Remember, no one was around, no one was watching, no one would know…if I did have a drink. Did I make the best decisions…even on day one? Probably not. I found myself going to three different bars where I knew the bartenders. I didn't order a drink, but was looking for conversation. So…I was "loose" on the streets of San Diego for night one, and I *didn't* have the drink that would have done me in. Success!

Over the next few days, I went to the morning group meetings hosted by my insurance carrier with the hopes of getting the referral to a rehab facility, and each day…I chose not to drink. It was MY decision and MINE alone to continue to be sober. When it got right down to it, it was MY mental fortitude that would prevail. I was beginning to learn that if *I* had the mental strength to do this, so do *others*. Maybe people just need a reminder from time to time, and to me that's what support is: being reminded and inspired by others' successes.

> If I have the mental strength to do this, so do others.

I reached out to a couple of acquaintances, and because of my sobriety, they turned out not to be friends at all. I wanted them to know I was staying at a hotel for a few days and wanted to get together for lunch. I just really felt I didn't want to be alone. I had been alone for a couple of weeks and the isolation of sitting in the hotel in between the hour and a half meetings I was attending was getting difficult. It turned out, neither of these people wanted to get together. They thought I'd preach to them and discourage them from drinking…they were both big drinkers. Nothing could have been further from the truth…I just didn't want to be alone. But, that's the way it was for the next few days.

It became evident that the particular route of rehab I thought was going to happen, just didn't present itself. With each passing day, I knew I could walk into any bar or liquor store I wanted to, because *I* was the one in charge of my actions. I found choosing not to enter those places was completely empowering. I knew I had "flipped the switch" in my mind and I was no longer a drinker. This switch for me totally exists. I knew it did, because I had found a similar switch that I turned off when I quit smoking. The counselors from the group meetings warned me about being so confident, as according to them, up to 80% of people relapse at some point. Looking back,

I really wish they would have educated me and the other attendees more on the 20% that didn't. I thought that was such a negative way to approach things, but I had to remember they had seen people encountering sobriety for the first time come in and out of there for years. But, I knew something else: they hadn't seen ME before.

Mentally, I was in control. Physically, I had done some major damage to my internal organs. I was still taking antibiotics for the *C. diff,* and that would continue for six weeks, plus I exhausted easily. At this point, I had to come up with a way to continue to work on the mental side of things, while developing a plan to strengthen physically. With nearly a week gone by, attending meetings, and being alone at the hotel, I decided it was time for me to come off of the road and get my own place again. Just to be safe, I wanted to choose a location near my primary care physician in San Diego, so I set the plan in motion. I would fly back to Phoenix to gather my belongings at my friend's house, then back to San Diego.

17

What a Long, Strange Trip It's Been

October 2011 (San Diego, CA)

I DID IT! I was back *home*. What a strange trip to get back to the city where I *had it all* just six years ago. I had my own apartment now, and I could decorate the way I wanted. I could come and go without feeling shame or guilt. I could enjoy the fresh ocean air of southern California. This time...I'd make it different. No longer a smoker and recovering from years of drinking, I was sure I'd be welcomed into the city with arms wide open. The catch...all my friends and acquaintances from six years ago had moved on. But, how tough could it really be to start over? Especially, since I had such a great story to tell. *But, who would I tell it to?* Without an existing friend base, my isolation continued.

What's significant in all of this alone time was the pure boredom I faced. They say boredom and isolation are big factors that drive people to end their sobriety, going back to drinking or their addictions. But, I was not going to *go out this way. I was not going to fail.* I was not going to have anyone know that I failed...so quite simply, I decided I would succeed! So, to distract my

> No, I am not going to fail, so I've decided to succeed!

brain and myself from the isolation and sitting in an empty apartment, I found that getting outside and enjoying my surroundings worked for me the best.

The first couple of weeks were really the hardest, because I focused on going to addiction meetings. In these meetings, not everyone was there to *get better*. It was pretty obvious who really wanted to quit a habit that had held them back in life and who was there to "mitigate" a situation. For example, there were people who were there to really embrace sobriety, but there were also those who simply wanted to avoid jail sentences or to minimize their use, and I could see who was who. I didn't judge. It was just something that I noticed. I *did* see the value in the support system and being around other people who were *in addiction*. My hope was that everyone there would decide to conquer their addictions, take personal responsibility, and show self-control to make changes in their lives. That wasn't always the case. Either way, I was continually encouraged to keep developing I Finally Quit, Inc. In actuality, the only "developing" that had been done was a prototype of the new logo and a lot of ideas. I still didn't know how to bring any of this out of my mind and into the real world…yet.

The first couple of weeks in San Diego were difficult, but I began changing my physical behavior. It all started with getting out for walks. In the beginning, the most I could go was about 6 blocks at a time. And, although completely exhausted, I wanted to be outside. I wanted to get some exercise, and this was really not like me at all. When I was drinking alcohol every single day, I avoided exercise like the plague! I couldn't believe how much change was going on within me. It was almost overwhelming. Not just the sobriety (that in and of itself was huge), but on these walks and going to these meetings, there was a lot of healing taking place, physically and emotionally.

With each passing day of sobriety, I was more and more

confident that I had overcome drinking. I didn't want to be overconfident at this point, but the mentality and my thinking at this time was very similar to when I quit smoking for good, just five years earlier. I knew I had flipped that switch in my head, and I was no longer a drinker. That was actually the easy part. The difficult part was filling my day with other activities. When it got right down to it, I had spent a lot of time each day focused around getting, drinking, and hiding alcohol. I began to feel a strong desire (and also an obligation) to get back to work.

It was nearly impossible to get my Type A inner voice to calm down and *appreciate* the time off from work I had right now. It had now been six or seven weeks since I had worked. I kept reaching out to my employer letting them know that I was ready to get back on the road and ready to get back at it. However, they had other plans for me. They kept telling me that I had to prove myself. I had to be sober for at least 30 days before they would consider putting me back out on the road. They kept telling me that it was for my own good, and wanted to make sure that I was healthy first. The truth was they had really lost confidence in me, and doubted whether I could be trusted to be out on the road. I had ruined all the good faith I'd built up over the years. Without being given the opportunity to get out and earn money, I wondered if this was some type of punishment.

Yes, that's it. I was feeling punished by my employer, and they were trying to prove the point that they were in control and not me. The feeling of punishment was being replaced by resentment. Resentment, anger, and *woe is me* are not great mindsets to be in when making a major life change and moving away from drinking alcohol on a regular basis. It would have been so easy to just cave and give in to the inner voice that piped up every once in a while. *Why not drink? No one really cares about you. No one comes to visit. You rarely receive calls or texts. Just go down to the store and get a bottle already.* My isolation continued.

Resentment is not a healthy place for anyone to be. For me, in the past, I would want to drink that feeling away. I kept trying to find ways to distract myself and not go down to the liquor store. The fear instilled in me by the medical staff back in San Francisco was slowly lessening, and I began to feel I wouldn't necessarily die if I drank. But, with each passing day, my desire to stay sober was being reinforced. Each day, I reminded myself I could and would survive without booze. I decided to embrace the fact that I wasn't working. And, I began to realize the blessings I actually had in life. Thankfulness started replacing resentment.

> With each passing day, my desire to stay sober was reinforced.

Just a few short years ago, I was homeless and living off of a food budget of just $10 per week. Now, I'd built up enough residual income in my *second* job to be able to afford not to travel. Sure, my finances may be tight if I never went back to the seminar business, but I could still handle the financial responsibilities of living in Southern California and maintain my own residence. As that epiphany was being celebrated, I had a major physical breakthrough, as well. I was able to put the cane down and start actually walking a mile or a mile and a half on my own without the support of the cane. Just a couple of days after that, the strangest thing happened...my walk turned into a jog.

This created the weirdest internal struggle ever. I couldn't stop my body from running, but my brain was questioning what was happening. *Why am I running? What's going on?* It was kind of like the scene in *Forest Gump* when he begins to run and his support braces break away from his legs. *Run, Forest, run!* So it was with me…I was running! In all honesty, my first "run" was all of about 30 feet before I was winded and had to stop, but my mind and body wanted more. I was getting stronger…I was getting healthier.

18

On the Road Again

December, 2011

My new commitment to myself extended beyond simply *not drinking alcohol*. I became committed to strengthening my physical well-being. As someone who was now almost 40 and never had a real workout regimen, I wanted to get in shape. Getting rid of cigarettes and alcohol really did clear my thinking. The thought of a gym or any type of structured routine was daunting. I had no idea where to start. An acquaintance of mine connected me with a trainer who owned his own workout equipment and weights. I was excited to get started.

Upon the initial visit with him, I held nothing back and told of my recent hospital stay and physical status (or lack thereof). I candidly told him that even though tall and 200 pounds, I felt as if I had the upper body strength of a 9-year-old girl. The point I wanted to stress to him was that I was incredibly weak, and not only had no upper body strength, but no core strength either. He was excited to get to work, as I would be his first "real" client. I'd come to find out this arrangement wouldn't necessarily be the best for either of us.

As we focused on building upper body strength, no attention

was paid to core strength or diet. We were just a couple of "dumb dudes" lifting weights. He devised a workout plan for me to follow on the days we worked together, as well as for the days that I'd be on the road. Yep, it was finally time to get back to work. I had proved to my employer that I was reliable and no longer drinking. They felt confident in sending me out, and I felt excited to get back on the road. I was supposed to travel on an intermittent basis, easing back into life on the road. The plan was for me to work every other week, giving me time to rest and continue with my new routine of working out and group meetings.

That plan quickly changed. During my initial employment with them from 1999 to 2005, then coming back after my homeless period, I had been one of the top producers for the company. Because they kept me off the road as long as they did, the financial impact had affected me and (presumably) the company. They quickly modified my travel schedule, sending me out for three weeks during my first month back.

Being sober and travelling across the country was eye-opening. I thought back to how I'd pour straight bourbon into a glass just to work up the courage to drive. I found that I wasn't afraid of *anything* anymore! I thought about the copious amounts of booze I would drink during my long drives from city to city. Now I took in the sites along the way.

My commitment to myself and the company was unwavering. There was no more booze, I was working out, and I was back to making money. I continued to stay sober, and gone were the days of travelling with a bag full of miniature alcohol bottles, multiple flasks, and sneaking booze at every turn. I was doing cardio on elliptical machines and lifting weights. The downside of the weightlifting was that I did not know what I was doing yet, and I didn't have any supervision from my trainer while travelling. I was sticking to my trainer's workout plan though, and it gave me more energy.

People in my seminars picked up on my energy, which quite frankly was intoxicating in itself. I WAS THRILLED TO BE ALIVE. I felt great and it showed. I loved telling people I was in the best shape of my life – physically, emotionally, and financially. It was almost as if the last seven years had been erased. Well…sort of. I was no longer drinking and had my own place again, but gone were the friends – the very people that made it fun to fly home.

> **I was THRILLED to be ALIVE!**

With my new upbeat and enthusiastic outlook on life, I was sure I was on my way to great things – I just knew it. Perhaps, what happened next shouldn't have caught me by surprise, but it sure is amazing how quickly things can turn. I was working in Florida and had already set my meeting room up for the next morning. With some time to kill, I decided to head down to the gym. In this particular hotel, to make it to the gym, I had to pass by the bar in the lobby during happy hour. I had been consistently walking right past gyms looking for bars in hotels for years. Now it was the other way around!

As I made my way to the fitness center, I had a feeling that I would really be able to make my idea of I Finally Quit, Inc. work. *It would be so cool to not have to travel for someone else anymore*, I thought. After my normal 20 minutes on the elliptical machine, I was poised for a quick bout of weightlifting. My first major setback since being sober came just minutes later. With very little to no core strength, I tore my abdominal wall while lifting. I knew instantly that this was the beginning of a hernia, because I'd had one nearly ten years earlier that required surgery.

The winner mentality I'd always had with the seminar

business, combined with the failure memories of the ICU, made me push my body to the limits. I knew the seminar company had taken a financial hit with me not on the road, so I kept my injury to myself for several weeks. When I finally did tell the company about my need to come off the road for a quick surgical repair, I was met with tons of resistance. The other seminar leaders who had filled the void for my last leave of absence were still enjoying getting time off the road. The owner of the company laid such a heavy guilt trip on me, I continued to work and travel five days a week for the next five months, before I finally scheduled the much-needed surgery.

The surgery was on a Tuesday, and I was right back on the road the following Monday. I knew I was giving way too much of *me* to the job and putting myself at risk for relapse. Every passing day that I wasn't working on this book, the "I Finally Quit" business plan, or website ideas (I still had no idea how to create the site), became problematic for me. After all, I really wanted to change the world. The feelings of resentment toward my employer this time around came because they kept me *on* the road so much. However, I was able to work through those feelings, process them, and let them go, which was incredibly life-changing for me.

19

Home Sweet Home

September 2012

Toward the end of 2012, I would make the decision to leave the seminar business. The company that had contributed to some of the highest of highs and lowest of lows in my life would become part of my past. And though I am very grateful to that company and my colleagues, it was time to move on. The thought of replacing that income was incredibly scary. I'd worked so hard to get it back, and now, just a few years later, I was walking away from it...again.

I would continue to work from home for the software company and build on the residual income. It was barely enough to cover the bills really, but I got to be home. Without the constant hassle of traffic, taxis, airplanes, and check-in lines at airports and hotels, it was amazing how much more time I had in my day. Gaining the freedom to work from home and making my own schedule would prove to be instrumental in furthering the IFQ movement.

I hired a *certified* personal trainer to work with me who understood where I was starting from and where I wanted to go. I stayed true to myself and chose a lifestyle that was healthier and brought me peace.

I worked harder than ever, persevering to be the best person I can be, and now I can proudly say:

I Finally Quit!

20

Where Do We Go From Here?

2013 and 2014

Over the course of 2013 and 2014, I continued to work on my physical, mental, spiritual, and financial health. The physical side of things (surprisingly enough) is the easiest to keep up with. Once I found a routine that worked for me, I've been able to stick to it. Polar opposite of "me" at the beginning of the book or eight years ago, now I find there is always time to get a quick workout in. I'm amazed at what just 20 minutes a day a few times a week can do. It's just 20 minutes! Did you know you can run a couple of miles in that time? Did you know you can do other cardio, like stairs, walking, elliptical machine, weights, or other quick workouts? I didn't, but now I do. *Me*, the guy who avoided nearly *all* physical activity even completed a 40-day run challenge in 2014, running at least 1 mile every day!

The mental side of my addictions are still there. I rarely think about drinking anymore, but if I were to be completely honest with you (why stop now, right?), there's been a day here and there where I thought about having a beer or a glass of bourbon. That's all they are though...just passing thoughts, and they can keep right on going by. Taking action on drinking is not something that interests me anymore...*been there, done that.*

The compulsive side of my personality remains, for sure. Nowadays, I obsess over every detail of I Finally Quit, Inc., from writing this book, to every edit, addition, or subtraction to the website. I'm constantly thinking of how to make a better "quitting" experience for anyone who registers at ifinallyquit.com. There's been more sleepless nights than I care to admit, as my brain races from topic to topic. I remind myself all the time that quitting is not a bad thing to be addicted to.

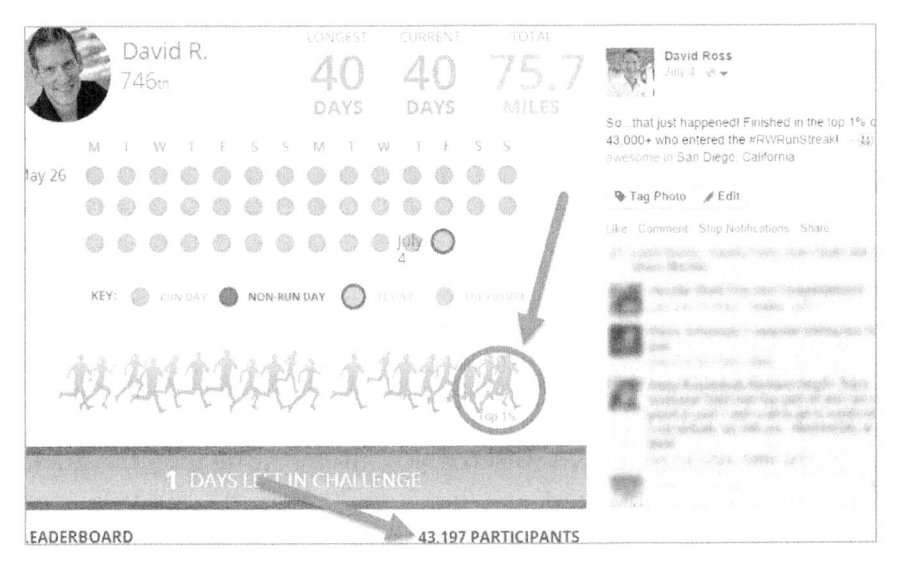

My spiritual life could still use a pick-me-up. There's always something going on at church or in the community, and someday I hope to give more time and money to causes. I really like it that I no longer have my travel schedule to blame for missing a service or event. It makes me much more accountable, so that makes belonging to a church easier for me.

Financially, well...I continue to work at securing my future. For nearly two years, I've put every extra penny into furthering the IFQ movement. Building a social community of people who want to inspire and be inspired, never giving up, and creating positive change in the world has been both exhausting and exhilarating for me. I'm truly amazed at how much time and money I've put into development, software, legal fees, consultants, coaches, editing, and more. I have spent more than six figures on all this, but to see people post on the wall inside ifinallyquit.com or purchase a t-shirt or other IFQ merchandise makes it all worth it.

The good news is I have every day to continue to grow and become the man I want to be. Physically, mentally, spiritually, and financially, I'll get there one step at a time. I know I have a long way to go, and I hope you all will join me along the way. I need you. Others need you. Please join the movement, and help me get the word out. People need hope, and they need to know that it is perfectly acceptable to say, "I Finally Quit!"

Epilogue: Thanks...

I'd like to personally thank you for purchasing this book and taking control of your life. With every purchase, the community of quitters grows, and I am further encouraged and excited to know people are changing their lives for the better. I have found almost everyone has at least one thing they would like to change about their lives or their behavior, with the final goal to be able to triumphantly say..."I Finally Quit."

Some have already done it, whereas some are still working towards quitting. Either way, hopefully this book will or has encouraged and inspired you to reach your quitting point, while learning to inspire others along the way. In order to do that, you'll need to be congratulated, encouraged, and challenged, so let me be one of the first...

I'd like to *congratulate* you! You are awesome! Many of us seek change in our lives, but do nothing about it. One of the hardest things as humans is to take action. Ultimately, it is action that leads to change. However, our internal dialogue usually prevents us from taking the first step. Just the simple fact that you picked up this book shows you are on your way. So again, congratulations.

I'd like to *encourage* you. I hope you have been transformed somehow while reading this book. I hope you feel empowered, and that you continue to make choices that lead to remarkable changes throughout the rest of your life. Keep in mind, this is not a quick-fix program. This is simply my unadulterated story of how I quit. My methods and situations may work for you and they may not. I share my story to inspire and get you to think. Whether you do exactly what I did or not (feel free to alter my methods slightly or altogether), just know you CAN quit any action or behavior. You have it within you. Quitting for me was a marathon, not a sprint – meaning it took time. If you are like me, when it comes to self-realization and making changes in your life, nothing is easy, but it *is* doable.

> I'd like to congratulate you, encourage you, and challenge you.

I'd also like to *challenge* you. I hope my story has challenged you to look at yourself, your situation(s) or those of a friend or loved one in a different light. None of us have it *all* figured out, but if you are like me, you want to be better, more complete, or just plain nicer to our fellow humans on this little rock in the universe. We all can make this a better place to live, and I challenge you to go out of your way every day to help, inspire, or encourage someone. Having a purpose beyond ourselves can keep us moving forward.

Lastly, I hope you enjoy quitting and the support you will find from unlikely sources. I like to tell people *quitting can be fun*. At first blush, people think that there is no way quitting can be fun, especially because it involves change. Change is one thing many of us humans despise. There's a phrase that comes to mind that I've heard many times in life: "I know what I like." Personally, I think it would be more accurate to say, "I like what I know."

Change is scary and it can be difficult. Taking on my personal changes and wanting others to have support during theirs are also reasons I taught myself html code and how to build a website that deals with quitting. Like a painter who has a beautiful work of art in their head, I had to figure out how to get it onto canvas. I had to learn how to get ifinallyquit.com onto the World Wide Web. It's there now, helping people achieve their *quitting* goals.

We all need support at some level. Some need more than others, while some get by with very little. You have something in common with your fellow humans out there. Keep an eye out for that person carrying a copy of this book, wearing that lapel pin, or someone who has an IFQ logo t-shirt on. They are advertising to you and the world that they, too, have quit something that has held them back. Give them a wink or a nod, a pat on the back, or a quick conversation. You will be encouraged yourself and can offer encouragement to them, freeing them or lifting them up.

Actually, that is how the IFQ website is setup. You (and others) can:

1. **Join the community**
2. **Communicate/interact with others**
3. **Be inspired to quit something**
4. **Wear the logo**

It is my vision to see the IFQ logo be a globally-recognized symbol of empowerment for those who have quit something; for those who have left detrimental actions or behaviors in the past.

There is a place where you belong. I highly recommend you take the steps and join us at www.ifinallyquit.com. Courageously face the challenges that are presented to you, not just in this book, but in life. That is exactly what I did...happy *quitting* to you all.

With warm regards,
David "the quitter" Ross

What is the I Finally Quit Movement?

My vision for I Finally Quit, Inc. is straightforward and simple. I see the IFQ logo being as recognized world-wide as the pink ribbon is. I see people proudly wearing the logo on shirts, hats, wristbands, and more, letting those around them know they have made a commitment to change.

When it gets right down to it and the *rubber meets the road*, most of us have similar emotional wiring. We have ups and downs, triumphs and defeats, successes and failures, and either way, we keep on going. When we are down, sometimes we need a helping hand. If you are like me, sometimes reaching out to that helping hand is difficult. Pride and shame can get in the way. When we are up, sometimes we need a pat on the back. Not for pride, but for acknowledgement of overcoming a struggle.

When I quit smoking, I felt a huge wave of success run through my body, as I knew…beyond a shadow of a doubt…I Finally Quit! Not only did I want others to feel that same success, I also wanted to be recognized for it. I just conquered the 20-year foe of tobacco and nicotine. I wanted to tell my story, but not to just anyone. I wanted to tell those who still struggled or thought they could not overcome.

Nowadays, I'll wear a t-shirt, lapel pin, and wristband with the IFQ logo on it, and almost every time I do, someone will ask…"Hey, what did you quit?" The logo and phrase are great conversation starters. I can say, "I quit smoking after 20 years and drinking alcohol after 25 years." The #1 response I've received is, "Good job!" I cannot fully express how good that feels each and every time I hear it.

So, what is the *I Finally Quit* movement? I envision a couple out to dinner, a lone traveler walking through an airport, or someone going about their business, then someone from across the room sees the IFQ logo and thinks, *Hmmm, I wonder what they quit.* Ultimately, these people have a quick conversation, and they both leave better off. The "quitter" feels empowered and encouraged in their triumph, and the person who approached them feels encouraged that they, too, may be able to quit…something, some day…whatever it is they want. Who knows…maybe it will be *you*!

Join the movement, interact with others, become a quitter, and wear the logo. There is no telling where we can go and who we can bring along with us.

About the Author

David Ross had a successful, 15-year career advising some of the nation's top executives, and leading seminars in all fifty states on healthcare industry topics. He was engaged, earning a great income, and had many friends. But due to serious addictions, by 2006, and for the next five years, he was homeless, scared, and alone.

Nearly dying due to alcoholism turned his life around – out of addiction and into a life driven by a strong passion to help others.

David is the founder and CEO of "I Finally Quit" and leads a growing and vibrant movement to support others who want to end bad habits and addictions once and for all.

Join us today at www.ifinallyquit.com.

I FINALLY QUIT

RAISED PUBLISHING AND PRINTING COSTS WITH

KICKSTARTER

ALL THANKS TO THE FOLLOWING PEOPLE:

Platinum IFQ Supporters

Stacy Ford - Spencerville Fitness

Dusty & Angi Hill

Diane Schumann

Tammy B.

Mitch Clauser

SmartIT Inc.

Institute for Mastering Success

Jarud Nash	Stephanie Ross
Kent Cravens	Kelli C. Holmes
Sunita Winchester	Stacy Glancy
HeadacheComfort.com	Jason Crook
Jodi Yoder Phillips	Tony McFee
Amy A. Owens	Jason Jauregui
Rodrigo Perez Mendoza	Kelly Allred
Amanda Minch	Anna Jennings
Brian Gibson	Tony Drexel Smith
Tricia Howard	Kickstarter Nat
Terilee Harrison	Katie D.
Jeremy & Erin Tisland	Whitnie Marie Twigg
Johanna Sandoval	Sean Leffler
The Crismans	Tayde Soto
Julie Dove	Amy Zimmer
Caren Eichel-Smith	Mike Conley
Mike Francl	Scott & Michelle Garibay
Teresa Vorhees	Scott Wiser
Jenny Wolf Dubach	Jessica Faurote
Peggy Jo Holly-Strickland	Jen Hamilton
Bryan Banville	Sharon Roberts
Ivy Ross	Suzanne Davidson
Heather Kongar	Dianna "DeeDee" Cook
Yasmin Rodriguez	Cheryl Siscon
Brett Jacobus	James Stewart

Creative Force Press

John "a fellow quitter" Gaudette

The Strait Family

Angi "Toots" Sprunger-Teeter

Zand Inc.

Jennifer (Mosser) Zimmerman

Beverly Smith

I Finally Quit...And So Can You is proudly published by:

Creative Force Press

www.CreativeForcePress.com

Do You Have a Book in You?

Friend, my sincerest hope is that you enjoyed this book as much as I enjoyed writing it.

Please share your thoughts by leaving a review.

Love the book?
Share your experience

http://bit.ly/IFQReview

Who Do You Love?

If this book touched you, inspired you, encouraged you and has motivated you to quit any "bad" habits, please spread the love and share it .... WITHOUT giving away your copy.

Detach And SHARE This Coupon
With Someone You Love

Give 15% OFF

♥

The book changing the way people quit "bad" habits!

Use Coupon Code LOVE at
www.ifinallyquit.com

Detach And SHARE This Coupon
With Someone You Love

Give 15% OFF

♥

The book changing the way people quit "bad" habits!

Use Coupon Code LOVE at
www.ifinallyquit.com

Made in the USA
Columbia, SC
11 May 2019